FINDING YOUR FEET
AFTER FUNDAMENTALISM

DARRELL LACKEY

APOCRYPHILE
PRESS

Apocryphile Press
PO Box 255
Hannacroix, NY 12087
www.apocryphilepress.com

Copyright © 2022 by Darrell Lackey
ISBN 978-1-955821-80-3 | paper
ISBN 978-1-955821-81-0 | ePub
Printed in the United States of America

Scripture references are from various translations as noted but otherwise from the English Standard Version (ESV).

CONTENTS

ACKNOWLEDGMENTS & DEDICATION

I want to thank my editor/publisher for approaching me, taking the time, and giving me so much incredible help and encouragement. John Mabry's winsomeness, humor, and intelligence are the perfect mix for what he does, and he does it well. I also want to thank my primary personal editor, my sister Rebecca Byrne, for making everything I write, better. And not only my writing, but my life too. Many thanks to several other editors as well for being so kind to edit many of the essays that appear in this work.

I must also thank and acknowledge Fr. Tom Brindley[1] and our merry band of gypsies (you know who you are), those fellow travelers, who live on the bridge, betwixt and between orthodoxy and many flights of fancy. Homeless in some ways with regard to religious tradition, our Sunday evening group has walked together now for many years, talking out back, in the alley, by the dumpster (inside joke). So much of my journey and this book are partly because of those conversations, started a long time ago, during those ocean fog covered evenings in West Marin, Northern California. Fr. Tom, you, in so many ways, are my spiritual father, mentor, and maybe most importantly of all… just…my friend. I am grateful.

I also want to thank my mother, Ruth (Bunn) Lackey. She was a voracious reader. Our house was filled with books and she set the example. I know where my love of reading and books came from.

Lastly, I want to thank my spouse, Shelly. She told me a long time ago, "You should be a writer—you should write books." I don't know if this is the book she wanted me to write, but I finally listened. She has always encouraged me, regardless, and that is no small thing.

This book is dedicated to Joshua, Andrew, Sarah, and Hannah. More than any book or work I have done, or could possibly ever do, they are the work of which I am most proud. And hardly my work alone. Only God's grace and their mother could put such a wonderful group together, in spite of all my shortcomings as a father.

Like most parents, I wish I would have known *then*, what I know now. I was wrong about so many things, including things of faith, of Christ, theology, and the Christian story. All I knew was fundamentalism/evangelicalism—what had been handed to me. Still, I was also a very immature person in early marriage and parenthood—I take full responsibility for that. I hope this book, in some minor way, makes some of that right. I am so proud of each of you. I love you more than could ever be put in words.

INTRODUCTION

What do we do when the bottom drops out? When there is no floor and we are free-falling, what do we grab on to? For many of us, that is how we felt when we walked away from our Christian fundamentalist world. I could also say the same of evangelicalism. I am well aware of the academic, theological, and historical differences, but anecdotally, and knowing what I grew up in, sometimes there isn't much of a difference. Either way, it can feel like living in a perpetual spiritual vertigo after leaving those worlds.

Many are calling the process of leaving that world: deconstruction. In this context, it has to do with taking the structure of fundamentalism/evangelicalism apart, brick by brick, as it pertains to the place we lived spiritually, theologically, and culturally. It's a rebuilding process. We've come to the place where we know the house, the structure we once inhabited, is no longer safe, true, or tenable. So, we need to rebuild, but before we do that, we have to examine the prior structure. Some of the material perhaps we can still use. Some of it, we may need to discard. I would add that deconstruction should be a positive process of rebuilding; it's not a destructive process of simply sitting around in the ruins.

Putting the deconstruction aspect aside, it is still extremely difficult (if not impossible) to completely leave the worlds that formed us from early ages. It's not as if we can wish the past away or start over as if it never happened. It did. And, for me anyway, not all of it was negative. Most of us, at the least, were introduced to the Christian narrative, no matter how flimsy or shallow the understanding. If one is starving and someone offers bread, even if we learn later that their theology or history was complicated (to say the least), we can still be thankful for the bread.

I try and separate the failures of the tradition—which all traditions have—whether of history, belief, or practice, over centuries, from individual people who happened to be born into and raised up in those traditions. And in my life anyway, many of them were very good people. I can remember many Sunday school teachers, deacons, pastors, and people from my early years who were wonderful, kind, caring, and important parts of my upbringing.

My point is that this journey isn't about leaving our past but understanding it differently and in a way that doesn't allow it to have a continued negative power over our lives. Easier said (written) than done, I know. I know for many, those years were toxic and abusive. I get that. For now, let's focus on where we are right now. This book is for those who grew up in, or had a significant history with, the world of Protestant Christian fundamentalism/evangelicalism in all it's different varieties (meaning, Charismatic, Pentecostal, Calvinist, Arminian, or even mainline subsets).

So, we've left that world. How, then, do we think about and practice our faith now? How do we inhabit the Christian narrative now? The way I have chosen to address those questions is somewhat indirect or elliptical. This isn't a "how to," book. Nor am I trying to just present new knowledge or information. My hope is that the reader will experience a different sensibility and perspective in the way I address many different subjects and topics.

I've maintained a blog for several years now, and I'm also a contributor to Patheos. This book will be an anthology of my blog posts/essays. I will preface each chapter with what I think these blog posts speak to and address. I should add that most of these posts have been revised and edited, for both grammar and content since first being published.

One of the keys to my leaving the fundamentalist/evangelical world, was my introduction to an ancient understanding of the Christian narrative that located it as something mystical and poetic, rather than something similar to a science or body of knowledge and facts. And I was introduced to this understanding, first, through my interactions with other Christians, who, through their lived lives, revealed just such an understanding of the Christian faith. Only secondly was it something I began to process intellectually. My heart had to "hear" it first through a lived and shared experience before my head could begin to see it too.

Thus, the nature of this book. What I hope to get across isn't just another theology, worldview, or way to intellectualize about something, but the sensibility behind it, the poetics, the sense of being in the world differently. While that may seem abstract and not very practical, I would suggest it is both, paradoxically. It will matter in your very real, everyday life. However, it is not going to seem very practical because we've been raised on the practical, managerial, how-to guides and this will feel different. At least I hope it does.

I should also add the caveat that this book isn't for those who left fundamentalism/evangelicalism and moved into atheism, agnosticism, or some other non-Christian faith. If such was your journey, I wish you all the best. However, this book is for those who left that world but still love Jesus and the Christian narrative. The book is for those who still consider themselves Christians and at the very least hold to the ancient creeds (Apostle's, Nicene, etc.), but have come to a place where the fundamentalist/evangelical "home" is no longer a place they can continue to live.

The chapters are divided into various areas of inquiry or life. The blog posts/essays have been chosen to fit those areas. If you have been in free-fall or still feel that way, this book is for you.

INTRODUCTION TO CHAPTER ONE

As already noted, there are many fundamentalist/evangelical people out there who think if one leaves their understanding of the Christian faith, the person is leaving Christ, God, the Christian narrative, the Bible, and church. And, yes, there are in fact some who do end up moving into atheism, agnosticism, or some other faith—or none at all. However, that is not representative of what is considered progressive Christianity.

People leave the Christian faith for many reasons. Progressive Christianity isn't a "gateway" into atheism or some other non-Christian faith. Further, many of those who left the faith completely were not drawn away or tempted into such by a progressive Christianity, but rather were running away from a toxic and abusive "Christian" fundamentalism.

A progressive Christian can hold to the major Christian creeds (Apostle, Nicene, and Athanasian), believe that the Bible is authoritative/inspired, that Christ rose from the dead, that Christ is coming again, that miracles are possible, and also believe that issues like same-sex attraction and abortion are extremely complicated matters with no easy answers, that patriarchy is not woven into creation, that the Bible isn't inerrant, that the earth isn't 6000 years old, that a Christian doesn't have to be a Republican, and that America isn't God's chosen nation. An ethical, Bible-believing, and faithful Christian can hold all those beliefs together without fear of contradiction or compromise.

My point is that progressive Christianity (what I believe is actually just orthodox or mere Christianity—I try not to get hung up on the name-tag) is not another faith and it is not some place one ends up if they leave the Christian faith/tradition. In fact, it could be seen as a returning or homecoming, much like what the prodigal experiences in the gospel.

What actually was different for the prodigal son? Did he ever stop being the father's son? Did he ever stop being his brother's brother? Did the home that he left ever stop being his home? What changed was his perspective. He began to see things differently and "came to himself." It wasn't his faith or the fact of who he belonged to that had changed—it was his ability to see those things again, in a new way, that changed.

Imagine hiking a mountain trail. The trail slowly rises in elevation as it circles the mountain with a barely noticeable incline. We may feel we are even walking on flat ground, but in reality, with each step, we are rising imperceptibly higher. Periodically, we stop and look back down the mountain and notice the valley, landscape, trees, streams, and rivers we left behind. We stop again further up the mountain and look back again.

However, now, we notice even more. We can see further now, even beyond those first trees and hills we saw before. Has the land down below actually changed? Of course not, what's changed is our perspective. We can see more the higher we climb. That is all that is happening when we leave behind our prior understandings of the Christian faith. The Christian faith hasn't changed—it was there all along. Just like the father who patiently waited for the return of his prodigal son. The father didn't change. What's changed is us—our perspective.

That is what the essays in this first chapter are really all about. To leave fundamentalism/evangelicalism is not to leave the faith, the Bible, or Christian tradition, but to see those areas from a different perspective now. The Christian life is a journey —one we might imagine that takes us from the bottom of a mountain (life) upward toward God. Let's start walking.

CHAPTER ONE

SAME FAITH—DIFFERENT PERSPECTIVE

CERTAINTY IS NOT FAITH

One of my favorite verses in the Bible is in Mark's Gospel: "Immediately the father of the child cried out and said, 'I believe; help my unbelief!'"[1]

That pretty much sums up my Christian journey—at least, in the sense I understand "belief" or faith differently. As a fundamentalist/evangelical, I understood faith as knowing for certain. To have faith was to believe or know with certainty something was true or would happen as believed.

Do I even have to point out how such a view sets one up for disappointment? After all, what happens when one has faith the earth is only six thousand years old, and then learns otherwise? What happens when one has faith their prayers for the sick will bring healing, but the healing doesn't take place?

What can often happen is the person doesn't question their view of faith, they rather question their faith in general, their very belief in God or transcendence. As many have pointed out, Christian fundamentalism/evangelicalism may be one of the best incubators of atheists/agnostics ever assembled.

Faith is paradoxical, mysterious, and engendered in love and hope, not certainty. There is a reason St. Paul tells us only three remain or abide, faith, hope, and love. There is something similar about all three of those things: They all involve risk. Faith is risky. Hope is risky. Love is risky. What if our faith is misplaced? What if what we hope for never happens? What if we love, and our love is rejected or misgiven?

In the face of those, "what ifs," we cry out: Lord, I believe; help my unbelief! The big (biggest?) question of life is—will we risk? Related—will we be vulnerable? Will we love, even when we don't know if it will be received—especially by our enemies? Will we allow ourselves to be loved? Will we hope, even if we don't know if what we hope for will happen? Does our faith arise out of how we answer those questions?

Faith is never something happening in a vacuum. Faith is linked to love and hope. And all three are risky. What they are not linked to is certainty. Living life could be seen as learning to fly. As we stand on the brink of life, on the brink of all the decisions we make, both significant ones and those not so significant, we sometimes feel like we are standing on the edge of the Grand Canyon.

As we peer over the edge, we cry out, "Lord, I believe; help my unbelief!" But much has brought us to that edge. Love and hope have brought us there. We cry and we struggle. "God, what if I fall!?" There is risk. There is faith. Welcome to your life. Your move.

LOVE IS OUR EVANGELISM

I grew up being told that even if I was a decent, honest, kind, and loving person—if I wasn't verbally sharing the gospel with people on a regular basis, I was still not a...take your pick... good, serious, mature, committed, or obedient Christian. Even if it wasn't said out-right (and it often was), it was still certainly implied.

As one could imagine, this led to a lot of guilt. It also led to a forced, contrived, and awkward attempts to "witness," where I often, I'm sure, just made other people uncomfortable. If one was an introvert and not very articulate, or not a people person, then it could be excruciatingly difficult to be a young (or older too) evangelical under constant pressure to evangelize.

One of the more freeing and wonderful experiences of leaving that world was to understand that the best evangelism is love, not words. Words come last. Actions come first. A lived life trumps all. All the references in Scripture to verbal sharing are given under the assumption that one's life is already marked by love or aspects of love.

For instance, in 1Peter we read: "But in your hearts revere Christ as Lord. Always be prepared to give an answer to everyone who asks you to give the reason for the hope that you have. But do this with gentleness and respect..."[2]

Notice the assumption here. One is being asked why he has this hope. The person asking has noticed something different about this person—that they live and act as if there is hope. This hope springs from knowing in our hearts that Christ is Lord. On a side-note, we also see the person waiting to be asked, and answering only then, with gentleness and respect. The gentleness and respect part I've noticed is missing in many a rabid fundamentalist/evangelical presentation.

In fact, I've done that myself. When I was still in that world, we were encouraged to be bold and blunt. Since then, I've learned the Christian narrative is passed on through lived lives, lives that are marked, for all their faults, by love. There is our struggle. Our struggle is not coming up with better evangelistic strategies, but in learning to love. I still have far—far to go.

We don't have to memorize canned presentations or imagine scenarios where we can turn the situation/conversation into a platform for our verbal "sharing." We don't have to try and steer the conversation or try and turn every topic, every point, everything said spontaneously by anyone in the conversation, back to spiritual things.

We don't have to make it about us. Whether a funeral, marriage, birthday party, social gathering, office function, or chance encounter, when we tell our Christian friends how we "used" those opportunities to share our faith, we show our true hand. This was about us, not them. We couldn't listen, or hear, what any of those other people were telling us, we couldn't be sensitive to the moment, because we were too busy formulating our plan to bring up religious topics. Regardless their response, we were anxious to get back and tell the people we were truly interested in (other Christians like us), and wanted to impress, how we were "good" and "obedient" Christians by our "sharing."

In other words, we don't need to have an agenda. We can interact with others from a position of organic honesty, whereby our only motive is to be decent, honest, kind, helpful, just, and loving people. *That* is evangelism. *That* is sharing. That is allowing the Spirit to work in us, which is also what allows the Spirit to work out of us, touching others.

As we turn inward and allow the Holy Spirit to conform us to Christ, as we focus on this journey of birth, death, and resurrection, as we live out the footsteps of Jesus, the paradox is that those around us are saved by this witness, regardless of words.

It was put this way by an Eastern Orthodox Christian, St. Seraphim: "Acquire the Spirit of Peace and a thousand souls around you will be saved."[3] This is a mystery, but it captures the idea that evangelism is far, far more than a sales pitch, a testimony, or just a verbal sharing or witnessing. The Spirit of Peace only resides in the lives of those who have been transformed by love. Absent the Spirit, peace, and love, our words are just sounds—even if those sounds are trying to say something about

Jesus. Without the Spirit of Peace, we might as well be talking about the moon.

Most of us weren't verbally argued or talked into the Kingdom. And if we were, chances are it was done by someone whose life we had already been attracted to, admired, or were struck by in some way. It's the difference between listening and hearing. People will listen to someone talking to them about God, the Bible, salvation, and spiritual things, meaning—it will register in their brains. However, people will *hear* those same things when coming from a life transformed by love. It will then register in their hearts.

Whoever said it, "Preach the gospel at all times; if necessary, use words," it is still true. Get out of the guilt trip world of feeling like you have to verbally share the gospel with people in all places and times. Instead, know that you are sharing at all times and in all places just by being a decent, honest, kind, just, compassionate, and loving person.

If we are the opposite of those things, we are still sharing and witnessing. Every life is a witness. Every life is a sharing. Every person is a conduit of their heart's content. The world, the universe, is a linked space, a connected space. What we are —pours out into the universe. We can act as a pollutant, or we can act as a spring of fresh water. I'm too often a pollutant. At best, I muddy the waters. Again, I have far to go.

At least I know now that faith is not transferred, stirred up, or given in our words, our testimony or "sharing." This has been greatly liberating to me, and sobering, all at once. Except for some, it's fairly easy to talk and share. It's hard to actively love—whether one is an introvert or extrovert. I don't mean to make this into an either/or dichotomy. Words, spoken or written, can be extremely powerful—obviously. My point is the world I grew up in had a laser like focus on verbal communication. They did make it into an either/or dichotomy, much like everything else they touched. For far too many, this only led to guilt and forced awkward conversations.

I'm happy to bid both goodbye. There are already plenty of awkward conversations in life, enough for all of us. There's no need to add to all the guilt and awkwardness that will come our way regardless. Eastern Orthodox theologian Sergius Bulgakov writes:

"Faith cannot be communicated externally or mechanically like knowledge; one can only be infected with it—by the mysterious and untraceable influence of one person on another."[4]

CHOSEN AND ELECTED

In Deuteronomy we read: "For you are a holy people to the LORD your God, and the LORD has chosen you to be a people for His own possession out of all the peoples who are on the face of the earth."[5]

And in Ephesians we read: "He [God] chose us [elected us] in Him before the foundation of the world."[6]

Two significant themes, or assertions, in both Testaments is the idea of being chosen or elected, out of all the people of the earth. We speak of the Jewish people as, "chosen," and Calvinists speak of Christians as those who were elected, pre-destined to be such, while those who end up in hell, the non-elect, are those who were pre-destined for perdition. So, we have Gentiles and the non-elect. Both doomed to an unclean, unholy, "otherness," existence, regardless their choices. In one case, it is a matter of birth and ethnicity. In the other (both really), it is a matter of divine decree from before eternity.

I doubt I need point out the concern that such beliefs could lead to a sense of superiority or pride. There is probably no greater contributor to the "othering" of people different than us, or outside our understanding of "salvation," than the notion that we are special, and "others" are not—than that we were born for heaven, while others were born for hell. And not born for either because of anything we have done, but due only to holy fiat, the will of God. We were simply lucky.

However, I would like to consider the notions of being "chosen" or "elected" from a different perspective. And this perspective is hardly original but has been put forward by different theologians over the years (notably, Karl Barth).

Let us consider Romans: "Therefore, as one trespass led to condemnation for all men, so one act of righteousness leads to justification and life for all men."[7]

As "types" there is very good scriptural evidence, and from many theologians, that Christ is the only "elected" man and that Christ is the only true Israel. We might say that it is only Christ who is elected and only Christ who is chosen. And just as "Adam" was the representative "man" or humanity, so the Incarnation allows for Christ to be the true representative man, but who is without sin. And just as Israel failed to live up to their calling, Christ fulfills their role as well.

And if Christ is the only elected and chosen one, to what end is such a status put? He did not come to be served, but to serve. He especially singled out the poor, the down-trodden, those who were thought or assumed not to be "chosen" or "elected"—they were the purpose for which he had come. We often forget that the parable of the prodigal son is specifically directed to those who thought they were the "chosen" ones. The son who remains at home, who gets upset as to how his returning brother is treated, represents those who consider themselves "chosen" or "elected." That fact may (or should) give one pause before he brags or pontificates a theology of being chosen or elected.

The paradox of these ideas regarding being "chosen" or "elected" like the rest of the upside-down world that Christ introduces in his coming, is the reversal of fortunes if you will. It would appear that one—Christ—is chosen and elected, for all those who were not. Further, this suggests that these then, all these "others," all those who were not chosen or elected, were the reason for the choosing and electing of Christ. Why? To this end:

"For in him [Christ] all the fullness of God was pleased to dwell, and through him God was pleased to reconcile to himself all things, whether on earth or in heaven…"[8]

And, "as a plan for the fullness of time, to gather up all things in him [Christ], things in heaven and things on earth."[9]

Keep in mind that expression "all" things. What does "all" encompass? For all those who believe we should take the Bible at its word, or "literally," are you willing to take the "all" literally?

If all things in heaven and earth will be reconciled and gathered up in the elected and chosen one, then by his life, by his death, and by his resurrection we are elected and chosen. This is why, ultimately, there is no, "us" and "them"—no true enemy. All existence, all creation, was elected and chosen by way of his being elected and chosen—and this gathering up of all things in Christ.

We live in the slow-motion world of temptation, one of the greatest of which is seeing everything through a binary lens, black/white, us/them. In a fallen world, wisdom sometimes demands understanding that some still operate from hate and not love. And that "some" includes "us." So, we navigate that environment with laws, customs, and wisdom as best we can. However, we should never lose sight of the ultimate end of "all things."

This is why the gospel is good news for everyone, all things, and not just an "elect." Any theology that seeks to divide, to "other," to create an inside/outside, holy/profane, clean/unclean, saved/lost, two story universe of any kind goes against the sweep of scripture and the grain of the universe. A divided world, a binary universe, always ends up being bad news for someone. Usually, someone not like... "us."

CHRISTIANS: WE DON'T HAVE TO BAPTIZE EVERYTHING

One of the heresies of modern times is that we live in a two-story universe. Here below is the "natural"—the material, the physical—and the "supernatural" belongs to the upper story, the heavens, the spiritual, that world we can't touch or see. Of course, if one is an atheist, then it's all a one-story universe, pure material/physical, pure matter-in-motion, whether up or down.

However, Christian orthodoxy believes the entire universe, all existence, is, like the Incarnation, both. We agree with the atheist that there is only a one-story universe. However, Christians believe it is a created space, both physical and spiritual. It's rather simple: The physical creation is spiritual, is supernatural —which is to say, it is natural, it is material. To the either/or question, we respond: Yes.

This means there isn't a "secular" space or some neutral non-spiritual habitat, whether material, social, political, cultural, scientific, or any other category one cares to name. You don't have to agree with me. I'm simply stating what Christians have traditionally believed before modernity and its bifurcation of everything.

One of the greatest capitulations to modernity, to the secular, as manifested in a supposedly invisible hand and neutral market, is the idea we need to create Christian versions of everything. Christians consider themselves just one more sub-group living in a two-story universe, wherein we now compete in the marketplace for influence here "below," while we wait for heaven, up there, "above."

The dominant aspect of modernity, which is the rule of

mammon, capital, looks at all these competitive imitations of each other and thinks, "How cute."

Thus, we get manufactured "Christian" music, movies, art, writing, comedy, science, diet plans, vacations, health care, dating sites, politics, etc. We look for Christian plumbers and electricians. We look for the fish symbol to guide our choices. In conceding every area of life, thought, and endeavor to a heretical vision, we play along in a never-ending fantasy of supposed influence or market gain. This is not "out-narrating" the other stories. This is a capitulation to the dominant narrative of market capitalism in a supposed God-less space.

I'm not speaking to the issue of Christian kitsch, which is another matter. I'm speaking to the idea all these areas of life are compartmentalized and seen as the neutral material we can fashion into something that now acts as propaganda or a conduit to get our "message" out. The idea is to baptize everything, make it "Christian," and then try and re-market it.

More than a capitulation, it is completely backwards. The entire cosmos, being created, is already infused with the Wisdom of God, the Holy Spirit, or as the Orthodox put it in their prayers: "...the Spirit of truth, who is in all places and fills all things..." All cultural endeavor, work, and creativity already has within it the stamp of God's imprint as creator, no matter to what use it may be put or if such is even recognized or believed.

It's true as well that creation, because of rebellion, is also broken. Thus, it can certainly be put to bad ends, or be ugly and false. However, that doesn't change the matter of its being created, declared "good," and now redeemed, even if that redemption is both now and not yet, or eschatological.

As Sergius Bulgakov[10] has noted, the earth is the holy grail, as it was the chalice into which Christ's blood fell. So too, we could add, has the earth been baptized as it also drank in the water from his pierced side. To discover the grail is to look around. To wonder if something can be made "Christian," or baptized, is to wonder about something already accomplished. The earth is the Lord's.

Thus, we don't need to make Christian versions of everything or to baptize every cultural work. Baptism is only for people as we follow the rest of creation. We need only produce what is good, beautiful, and honest, regardless of whether it mentions God, the divine, or carries a fish symbol. Take that which is already baptized and simply make it what it already is when fashioned out of love and spun into something good, true, and beautiful.

Even if a work is meant specifically for Christians, such is more a matter of worship and formation than a specific version of something. After all, non-Christians, atheists, and people of other faiths can also produce that which is good, beautiful, and true simply as it relates to being human and sharing this existence.

Let the other narratives mimic and compete as the market and capital wink and count their money. Christians though should rather live in the *Real* (as opposed to the simulacrum world created by the market) and by their work and endeavors produce that which transcends themselves, the market, place or time, and becomes a treasure for everyone.

JESUS AND DRAGONS

I gather together, as often as I can, with a wonderful group of Christians who meet in a private home Sunday evenings. We go through the Eastern Orthodox liturgy together. Afterward, there is tea, fellowship, and then we discuss a book we are reading together. It is a wonderful, informative, challenging, and transformative experience.

Over the years, one of the most frequent topics to come up has been dualism. This is the idea of a two-story universe, where there is the material/physical "down here" and then there is a spiritual realm, somewhere "out there." This breaks existence in half really and it ends up touching on everything. It becomes the lens in which we interpret our world. This, in fact, is modernity.

For instance, we talked about grace and suffering. Pain and joy. And we discussed the idea that these are things better thought of as being together rather than separate. The point was made that we think of the crucifixion and resurrection as two different things, events, and moments. We think of it linearly, in time, as we would when watching a parade go by. However, perhaps they are the same. Perhaps, the crucifixion is the resurrection.

In thinking about this, I thought the same might apply to heaven and hell. Perhaps they are the same as well. What I mean to say is this: Rather than thinking about them as locations, spatially, separate spheres, or even linearly in time, maybe they are the heart responses to the same reality, which is Christ.

When Jesus descended to Hades (The Apostles Creed), heaven was in hell. When there was, "war in heaven",[11] hell, the dragon, was in heaven. Imagine, dragons (see what I did there), in heaven.

When I am in hell, Jesus meets me there. When I am in heaven, even there, war is/was possible. Pain and joy. Grace and suffering. Crucifixion and resurrection. Heaven and hell. Which is which? Or, where am I? Well...yes.

My prayer is that when we feel we are in hell, we know, at the same time, Jesus is on the way (which means he's already there). When we feel we are in heaven, we know, at the same time, that such might not be exactly what we thought it should be. Especially if a dragon shows up.

We think we know exactly where we are when we are either suffering or experiencing joy, but do we? After all, Jesus and dragons can show up in the most unlikely of places.

INTRODUCTION TO CHAPTER TWO

One of the defining features of American fundamentalism/evangelicalism is its eschatology. In fact, I would submit one cannot understand that tradition very well at all without digging into their eschatology—their view of the "end times."

The impact of their end times understanding has probably impacted almost every area of life in American culture. Two areas that come immediately to mind are the environmental and the political.

When a person believes there is an escape plan rather than a restoration plan, they see the world differently. One reason so many fundamentalists/evangelicals view environmentalists and environmentalism with suspicion, is because they see the world as temporary and, in a sense, disposable.

They also mistake a devotion to preserving and protecting creation as worship. Perhaps that is true for some, but such should never eclipse the fact every Christian is called to be a protector and preserver of God's good creation.

There is a wonderful passage in Harper Lee's wonderful and sobering book, "To Kill a Mockingbird."

"Sometimes the Bible in one man's hands is worse than the whiskey bottle in the hand of [another]…there are just some kind of men who' are so busy worrying about the next world they've never learned to live in this one, and you can look down the streets and see the result."

The dispensational/rapture/tribulation eschatology (DRTE) that dominated the fundamentalist/evangelical world for decades (and still does) is a very big reason so many of us were way too busy "worrying about the next world" and not taking care of the world right in front of us. How sad. Not only was the garden not tended, we hardly even enjoyed it. We were too busy staring upward:

"When [Jesus] had said this, as they were watching, he was

lifted up, and a cloud took him out of their sight. While he was going and they were gazing up toward heaven, suddenly two men in white robes stood by them. They said, 'Men of Galilee, why do you stand looking up toward heaven? This Jesus, who has been taken up from you into heaven will come in the same way as you saw him go into heaven'" (Acts 1:9-11).

Unfortunately, too many Christians are still standing looking up. That means no movement, no work, and no moving on. It means missing everything else going on around us. What the DRTE view did was to freeze generations of people into standing still and looking upward. Thus, the physical creation suffered and whenever she suffers, we all eventually suffer.

Along with fundamentalist/evangelical eschatology, their view of salvation and final judgment are, I have come to believe, fear-based rather than Bible-based. I find myself more and more coming to a hope that all may one day be saved, redeemed. I think there is more scriptural support for such a hope than most Christians realize. I also think there is more support from early church theologians for such a hope than most Christians realize.

We have often been led to see God as divided in mind and heart to a certain extent. On the one hand we are told that because of our sin, God hates us and will destroy us. However, this same God intervenes and saves us...from himself! Rather than seeing the Holy Trinity as the ontological basis for love, peace, and joy, this other view sees the Trinity as a dysfunctional family, where one parent protects the children from the other parent. Does that seem reasonable, ethical, or healthy? Is that good Christian theology?

I realize the view that all might be saved is a minority view. I'm not dogmatic about it. I don't see it as a core belief one must hold (Nicene Creed) to be considered orthodox. However, I think much of the dysfunction and fear I experienced in the fundamentalist/evangelical world, was due to their emphasis on things like a rapture and the eternal, conscious, torture of those considered not Christian.

Are there other ways to think about eschatology, salvation, and final judgment? I believe there are. This next chapter of essays will hopefully lead us in that direction.

CHAPTER TWO

SALVATION AND THE END
OF DAYS

PEOPLE, NOT PROJECTS: RE-THINKING EVANGELISM
(MORE THAN A CHECK LIST)

We need to re-think evangelism—what it means and what it should look like. The common Christian understanding of evangelism sees the world in a stark black-and-white of "saved" and "unsaved." We are "saved" and everyone outside our understanding of what that term means is "lost." This view of evangelism, in my opinion, is both destructive and un-Biblical.

When we view people as part of a black-and-white world, they become "projects" rather than people, who are, in many ways, just like us: people on a journey. It can make us approach people differently. In our consumer driven world, it can turn us into salespeople rather than friends. It can also engender a sense of superiority. We can begin to develop the attitude that the Pharisees, and the Jews in general, had toward Gentiles—the notion of them being "unclean" and less than God's "chosen" people.

The person we approach with this sensibility (project rather than person) immediately, or sometimes slowly, begins to sense a hidden agenda. It's not that we really want to get to know them, or just befriend them regardless, or that we are acting out of an innocent and pure display of love and caring. They begin to sense that we want to "sell" them something, and that our "friendship" is just a ruse to tell them about our religious beliefs. Often, if they are not ready or not interested, we soon drop them. We no longer call or show much interest in them. We move on to the next "project."

This is not to say that we should not share our faith, and it is not to say that some people recognize Jesus as savior, and some do not. But there is a complexity here that, rather than trying to understand, we often ignore. There are at least three reasons why we need to re-think the boundary between "saved" and "lost."

First, a continual theme in the earthly ministry of Jesus was his constant blurring of the boundary between the saved "Jews" and the lost or unclean "Gentiles." Jesus repeatedly challenged those (the Pharisees) who were so sure they were "saved" or "in," while they viewed all others as lost, unclean, or outside the sphere of salvation. This theme runs throughout the Gospels.

Second, we have the Magi.[1] These men were Gentiles, pagans, and astrologers. They were the furthest thing from what was thought of as "saved" in the minds of the Jewish religious leaders at the time and even now in evangelical or fundamentalist circles. And yet, these men saw and recognized what the "saved"—the "chosen"—did not see and missed: the birth of Jesus and that he was worthy of worship, that he would be king. They saw the signs of his coming and they traveled to him. When their lives were in danger, we are told they were warned in a dream. Who warned them? God did—God was with them. So, were they "lost" or "saved?"

Finally, in Acts, we have Paul's Mars Hill sermon[2], where he

tells the "lost" Athenians that even their very being is "in Him."
Even those we think are "lost" have their being "in Him." Their
"lost-ness" is complicated and blurred by the fact they are "in"
God and also not far from Him—at the same time.

A crucial part of the ministry of Jesus and what he tried to
teach his disciples was the idea that these categories and ways
of thinking (clear solid boundaries between "us" and "them")
are actually more porous and traversable than we realize. Many
of his parables seem to go directly to that point—the Good
Samaritan being a prime example.

I wonder what would happen if we shared our lives with
people first and loved them regardless of whether they ever
accepted our message or not? What if we protected them, fed
them, gave them drink, clothing, and encouragement simply out
of love, with no hidden agenda whatsoever? We would be living
our faith then and that is the only type of faith that saves. Not
only does it save others, it saves us.

Evangelicals and fundamentalists normally have a certain
criteria in mind for whether a person is "saved" or not. Whether
we realize it or not, we "hear" what others tell us about their
faith (or lack thereof) within a matrix of our own making,
wherein we silently, probably unconsciously, check off certain
mental boxes. We need to know the year or timeframe they
made a public commitment to Christ. Check. We need to know
their commitment was voiced (did they pray the sinner's prayer
or use similar language?) or made in line with our theological
beliefs. Check. We need to know it was made within a tradition
we agree with theologically (were they baptized correctly?).
Check.

When all the boxes (or most) can be checked off, we smile
and silently within ourselves grant them access into the
Kingdom or grant our agreement they really belong and are not
imposters. How nice of us. How big of us. We can rest easy now.
Of course, this is all very silly. We've all known people who

could check all the boxes and who have since left the faith or who live now as if they never even heard of it. Conversely, we know people who cannot pass the criteria very well, if at all, who nevertheless exhibit true love for Christ and others.

We need to let go of our checklists, our canned presentations, our arrogance that we are on the inside, that we are the gatekeepers deciding who may come in. Instead, perhaps we should pray and hope for a wide mercy—one that will allow even us, the chiefs of sinners, to be remembered on the last day.

Love has no agenda, other than love. Love has no hidden intent. Let's stop befriending people in order to share a message that is verbal only. Quit coming up with strategies to make connections with people simply to (verbally) sell them something. For each person that comes into your life, simply love them. Share your life. Share *you*. If Christ is living in you, if you are walking in the Spirit, if you are an imitator of Christ, then you are sharing Christ with them. If they want to know more after that, great. If not, that was never the point anyway–love was.

WE ARE SHEEP—WE ARE GOATS

In the Christian narrative we find the picture of humans and their response to God (lived lives) portrayed by the categories of sheep or goats. There are positive connotations associated with sheep and negative ones with goats. For example, Jesus tells about the "Final Judgment." We read:

"When the Son of Man comes in his glory, and all the angels with him, then he will sit on his glorious throne. Before him will be gathered all the nations, and he will separate people one from another as a shepherd separates the sheep from the goats. And he will place the sheep on his right, but the goats on the left."[3]

Those on the right, the sheep, are told to come and inherit

the Kingdom. Those on the left do not fare as well. Or, at least this is the common understanding of these verses. The sheep are bound for heaven, while the goats to eternal perdition. One is either a sheep or a goat, there is no in-between. Two groups. Very simple. Very black and white. You know, the way most of us like our theology.

And yet, I wonder. So too did Eastern Orthodox theologian Sergius Bulgakov. There are alternative readings to what we call the "final judgment," or the end times. Bulgakov offered such a reading, which I find compelling and closer to the over-all sweep of Scripture, the Christian narrative, and the God portrayed therein.

What partly formed his reading of Matthew 25 about the sheep and the goats, was his view of what "judgment" entailed and meant. We normally view judgment as something happening outside ourselves. We stand before an external judge who makes a decision regarding our lives, our souls. It is some-thing handed down to us, rendered or decreed. It is separate from our own judgment, reflection, or internal calculus.

Bulgakov saw it differently. He saw an encounter with Christ at the final judgment as a moment of self-judgment, an internal awakening and revelation. To stand before Christ was to see and understand, for the first time, the gulf, the chasm, the distance between who we were and who he is. It is a self-realization of profound depth. One looks in the mirror and finally all pretense, all falseness, all the masks, excuses, defenses, and every parti-tion of hiding are all now gone in the light of Christ's presence. We are completely naked and see ourselves for the first time.

When we internally experience the brute realization of what we are—compared with what we see in Christ, therein is our judgment. This doesn't mean we subjectively decide our own personal judgment or fate. In fact, for the first time, we will have a purely objective, honest, real, and true view of ourselves. If we now have even a glimmer of self-awareness or ability to reflect, such should give us considerable pause.

I would imagine we will be undone. It will be in that moment that, we, like David, will learn we are the "man."[4] We who cried, "Who did this?!" "Who is responsible for this?!" will learn that we did this, we are responsible. No more need be said. No external judgment can compare to the one that comes within and is now in agreement with the universe, love, the Trinity. The truth.

With that understanding of the final judgment, Bulgakov interprets the sheep and goats in Matthew 25. We read of the separation of people. When we think of the evils that have befallen humankind, they are almost always preceded by the separation of people. We categorize and designate the "other." We decide who is "in" and who is "out." All prejudice, much mistreatment and injustice, begins by the separation of people. This happens first in our hearts and then too often becomes a physical reality, enforced by either custom or law.

However, Bulgakov saw the separation happening in Matthew 25 not as a physical separation of people, but as a separation that happens internally, in our spirit and soul. We are each a sheep and a goat, all at once. We might say each will burn in hell and also experience the sublime heavens. Or, put another way, we will all stand before Christ. We read:

"The separation of the sheep and the goats, with their final destinies, is a figure that refers not to individual persons or groups of persons but, above all, to their inner state. The possibility of heaven and hell is present in every soul, although to different degrees. This is a horizontal division that passes through all humankind, not a vertical one, which would separate it into two mutually impenetrable parts...Therefore, the idea of two humankinds, divided and separated from each other at the Last Judgment, does not correspond to the fullness and connectedness of reality. Humankind is one. It is one in Adam and one is Christ..."[5]

These interpretive understandings along with others are, no doubt, what partly inclined Bulgakov toward universalism. What is it that we fear with such interpretations and understandings? Do we fear we are interpreting incorrectly, or is it something more?

I would imagine most of us want an outward judgment based upon locating a moment in time when we were "saved," or upon some outward, physical act like baptism or a good life. It must be somewhat unnerving to consider our judgment might be the inner revealing of who we really are, which is to say both a sheep and a goat. Further, that being such is a "line" running through every heart. As Alexander Solzhenitsyn reminded us:

"The line separating good and evil passes not through states, nor between classes, nor between political parties either—but right through every human heart—and through all human hearts. This line shifts. Inside us, it oscillates with the years. And even within hearts overwhelmed by evil, one small bridgehead of good is retained."[6]

Again, we will all stand before Christ. This is our judgment; this is our heaven and hell. We will then realize we are sheep and goats, we are saved and lost, all at once. Thus, we pray, Lord have mercy.

THE PRODIGAL SON AND HELL'S LOCATION

If we were to put aside the idea that hell is a geographical/physical or even metaphysical/spiritual realm, but rather a state of relative being, something we carry around in our hearts, the story of the Prodigal Son[7] may help us see its location in how we respond to, or understand, our place in the Trinitarian economy, both temporally and eternally.

This is a meditation and reflection. I'm not positing something doctrinal or systematic. This is more a poetics, or more likely something aporetic. This is a speculative and alternative reading of the Prodigal Son for sure. Still, I'm satisfied in my own mind and heart as to any conclusions.

The story of the Prodigal Son is deeply subversive in many ways, but especially of all narratives that posit a certainty of salvation or lostness based upon temporal locations, of who is "in" and who is "out" of the father's, the god's, or the spirit's good graces and favor—at any given moment in time. The story problematizes location (in various aspects) as being a certain or secure temporal foundation indicative of one's "salvation" or relation to the Father.

The narrative also seems to suggest that while both sons represent two opposing relationships with the father, neither's actions, or locations, overcomes the father's love for each of them. Both are welcome to remain in the father's house; both sons are told they are loved. Therefore, the heaven or hell each experiences is within them—it is not exterior to their actual circumstances of being loved and welcomed in the father's house. They are actualized only by their response to the father's love, but the father makes no other pronouncements or judgments upon his sons, other than those evidenced in his actions.

First, the son who leaves. Yes, physically he leaves, but does the father's actions allow room for a deeper understanding of "leaving?" Since the father sees his son from far off, was he always looking for his return? Was he always scanning the horizon? His broken heart is now large enough to hold his son there. If love never fails, if love is the most important thing to remain (1 Cor: 13), then his son has not truly departed. His son resides there, in the father's heart. Even though the son eventually feels he is in hell, he is not. He may be in the temporary purifying fires, but his true self is in heaven, his father's heart and home.

Second, the son who remains. Yes, physically he remains at

home. But notice he is not looking for his brother, like the father does. It would have been very upsetting to witness what his brother did and to live in the aftermath. We can almost feel his resentment and anger at his brother, which we eventually see when he responds to his brother's returning. It is this anger and resentment that indicates he has left his father's home as well, if not his father's heart. He too wanders, even if physically at home.

The son who leaves is many things. At the least, ignorant, impertinent, and immature. However, he doesn't seem to hold any anger or malice toward his father or brother. We aren't told why he leaves, but it doesn't seem to be for reasons of anger or hate. Thus, he too carries his father and brother in his heart—even in the far country.

It is difficult to say the same of the brother who remains. I wonder if in his anger and resentment, he had let his brother go (thus his true surprise at the return). If so, then it is he who has left and not his brother. To hold onto anger and resentment is to live in hell (which is to be in a far country and not home), regardless of one's physical surroundings—even in the paradise of the father's home. To live in ignorance, but still hold onto one's love for father and brother, is to carry heaven around, regardless of one's physical surroundings and even in spite of one's short-sighted choices.

We have two sons leaving and remaining in this story. We also have the circumstances of their leaving and remaining. However, we cannot locate (truthfully, ontologically, spiritually) either, based simply upon their physical location or temporal, finite circumstances or choices. We can only locate them in their response to each other (which holds the possibility of transcending the temporal and finite—because love remains; or conversely, in resentment, the creation of a finite space for further purification). In that sense, we find that the son who remained, was actually the one who truly departed. He had departed in his heart. The son who physically departed, in his heart, had actually remained.

Who then- is the prodigal? Who is "in" and who is "out?" We read:

"Now his older son was in the field, and as he came and drew near to the house, he heard music and dancing. And he called one of the servants and asked what these things meant. And he said to him, 'Your brother has come, and your father has killed the fattened calf, because he has received him back safe and sound.' But he was angry and refused to go in. His father came out and entreated him…"

Notice the "in" and "out." The son who remained, now refuses to go "in." He is outside now. However, the father comes "out." This love that refuses to let either son go, goes to each, wherever they are—and "entreats" them to come back "in" where they belong. Only we can stay outside—the father doesn't put us there. Only we can go to a far country, the father doesn't send us there.

Thus, the father's house is always open, and we are always welcome—only we ourselves can prevent (and only to a point) our ingress to the place, if we ever come to ourselves, we know is home. Our ability to do so, is entirely bound up in relation and our response to relation but not in our temporal, finite, location or circumstances (whether physical of spiritual). Hell is about relation and response, not our temporal location or the circumstances of our finite choices. In this sense, the consequences of our failures in the areas of relation and response, are the finite fires (hell) of purification burning off that which prevents us from being in right relation, from seeing and seeking the Good.

Thus, heaven and hell reside within and we carry each with us wherever we go, and they are activated or actualized by our response to the Father's love, but never the Father's judgment or command whether eternal predestination or pure absolute will in temporal time. If hell is an abode or structure of evil, then it is finite, as evil is not an ontological reality, but a privation, a shadow. Thus, it can never be determinative, into perpetuity, given our temporal, finite locations within the redemptive drama of creation and eschaton. And this would be true, regardless our temporal choices, because of the eternal love of the Father, which is the only ontological reality—that which truly exists.

However, in the summing up of all things, then we will find ourselves finally in the Father's house, where we were all along, in his heart. Now location, desire, the temporal, and the finite, will rest and join eternally in the peace, love, and infinite joy of the Father's presence—which becomes our final and only "location" or home. Where our hearts were always held, our glorified bodies will now join. Then, as St. Paul puts it:

> For in him all the fullness of God was pleased to dwell
> And through him God was pleased to reconcile to himself
>   all things
> Whether on earth or in heaven by making peace through
>   the blood of the cross.[8]

Without this reconciliation, we would have the possibility the father remains forever looking for the lost son, which would mean love fails. And it would posit that something exists more powerful than love—something as mundane as an immature, stubborn, and finite ignorance and will. It would also mean "all" things doesn't really mean "all."

Despite any hell and any purifying fires and judgment, which are no doubt part of our salvation, I believe Sergius Bulgakov was right: "It is impossible to appear before Christ and to see him without loving him."[9]

If a world existed—where the Father remains—eternally looking for a son who never returns, then such a world would be a hell. It is our eternal praise that such a world was never created or, for that matter, even possible.

THE OUTSIDE IS THE INSIDE

I was looking at a verse in the book of Hebrews this week regarding the location of Christ's death. Here is the verse: "Therefore Christ also suffered outside the city gate in order to sanctify the people by his blood."[10]

The Old Testament required two main types of offering. A guilt offering and sin offering. While the guilt offering (animal remains), once offered, could be left within the temple, the city, not so with the sin offering. Once the blood was used, the remains were burned, outside the city, outside the camp.

Since this offering represented the sin of the people, it had to be taken out, away, and separated from the community. To be put out of the community, and seen as sin or sinful, was to be shamed. It was to bear abuse and reproach. It was to be taboo. This was all represented by the remains of the animal sacrificed as a sin offering on behalf of the people.

What I am more interested in here though is location (sort of). If we think of ourselves as lost, sinful, shamed, bearing abuse and reproach, we think of ourselves as being, "outside." We are "outside" the church walls, community, faith, and fellowship. We are "outside" the gates of heaven. There is the community of the "saved" and we are "outside" that community. We are outside the city gates, outside the camp.

We are told the whole point, the goal of salvation, is to get "inside." We want to be inside the city gates, the camp. Inside it is warm and there is food, drink, and shelter. There is protection —strength in numbers. Here we are accepted and part of the community. Inside is salvation.

Here though is the problem: The only way to the inside, is through the outside. Further on in Hebrews we read: "Let us then go to him *outside* [emphasis added] the camp and bear the abuse he endured. For here we have no lasting city, but we are looking for the city that is to come."[11]

However, perhaps we should clarify: The "way" to the inside being through the outside, might better be understood as—the outside is the inside.

From verse 13, if we think of the "city" (this city could represent many things) "here" as our supposed salvation, we must always be going to him, who is outside this camp, outside this city. Here we have no lasting city. Jesus is always, until creation is restored, outside the city gates, outside the camp. And we must always be moving toward him, which is to move outside whatever city we currently think is our salvation, or in which we trust.

And whenever we leave the comfort of the city (this city could represent many things), which can never be the city we are waiting for, as we move "outside" its gates, outside that camp, we are actually on the inside now, because salvation was always outside with Christ.

Jesus is the eternal city, temple, and home—our sabbath rest. The outside is the inside.

GOING THROUGH OR ESCAPING FROM?

What does it mean to be saved from something? Further, does being "saved" from something exempt us from suffering? We use the word in many different ways. In Christian thought, there is the idea we were saved, we are being saved, and we will be saved. There is a past, present, and future sense to our salvation, so "locating" the event is problematic.

In that sense, where is the "saving" located? Locating salvation is difficult because it is not a static, once-in-time, type of event. That problematizes the fundamentalist/evangelical obsession with knowing the specific time frame (even day, month, and year) of a person's salvation. That mindset is what leads to the focus on personal testimonies, of being able to identify a specific moment in time- when a person was "saved." It is so important that many fundamentalists/evangelicals doubt a person's salvation if they cannot give that type of specific information.

When we consider the narrative arc of the Judeo-Christian story, we see that salvation is more a going through- than an escaping from.

While not exhaustive, here are some examples:

Noah and his family[12] did not escape the rains, nor the loss of home or the life they knew beforehand but went through the storm upon the grace of an ark.

Moses and the Hebrew people[13] did not escape the Red Sea; they went through the sea upon the grace of dry land.

Daniel and his friends[14] did not escape the furnace; they went through the fire upon the grace of God's presence.

Daniel did not escape the lion's den;[15] he went through the night with the lions upon the grace of God's provision.

The Apostles and first disciples of Jesus did not escape jail, imprisonment, or physical harm; they went through each instance upon the grace of knowing Christ's presence and suffering on their behalf.

Jesus did not escape the cross; he went through it all, from temptation in the desert, to his cries in Gethsemane, to his flogging, his crown of thorns, his cross. He went through this time, these events, carried upon his great love for all creation.

This constant Biblical theme of going through, rather than escaping from, is one of the reasons (among many!) that I let go the fundamentalist/evangelical belief in a Rapture of God's people to escape the judgment and suffering they believe is coming for all those not "saved."

The idea of a "rapture," an escaping, a being caught up or away from suffering doesn't seem to follow the Biblical pattern. It also doesn't ring true to life. Even as Christians, we suffer. We are not exempt. The rain falls on the just and the unjust. The sun shines on the believer and the unbeliever.

We don't escape the "valley of the shadow of death;"[16] we go through the valley because "you are with me..."

If salvation is more about *going through* than escaping, where do we locate our salvation in time? When does going through end on this side of the vale? And when we see the water, furnace, den, valley, or cross up ahead, where is our salvation located then? Were we saved when we crossed the dry seabed, or when we stepped to the other side? Were we saved when we were in the furnace, or when we stepped out of the furnace? Were we saved when we prayed with the lion's breath upon our face, or when we were pulled up out of the den? Were we saved before the valley, in the valley of the shadow, or when we felt the sun on our face as we walked out of the valley? And were we saved if we did not come up from the water, or den? Were we saved if we did not come out of the furnace or valley?

I think the answer to all those questions is: Yes. Salvation isn't a location or moment in time or an escape from time; it is our journey through time and eternity.

LORD OF THE LEFT-BEHIND

Growing up in the fundamentalist-evangelical world, along with the fear of a girl's rejection, test taking, and the general anxiety and guilt of enjoying "worldly" music, movies, and television, I also worried about being- "left-behind." In the late 70's, sermons, songs, Bible studies, and best-selling books were rife with the eschatological belief in a "rapture" of "true" Christians, while the unfortunate rest, the doomed, are, "left-behind."

There have been many books[17] and scholarly works over the

years debunking the eschatology underlying the belief in a "rapture," and currently it may be at its most weakened state, since its inception. For this decline we can be thankful. That one belief, along with its supporting theology, is a significant reason why so many evangelicals dismiss environmental concerns, support Israel no matter what, and display other destructive sensibilities.

Putting aside the Bible passages used to support a rapture and the theology that underlies it, what we often miss is the privilege it seeks to legitimize. It is a theology of glory and certainly not one of the cross. All such theologies are ultimately about privilege. Which is to say they are about believing one is chosen, over and above, others. These "others" become the "left-behind." We might even see the term, "left-behind," as a metaphor for our times.

Many don't have to wait for a future "rapture" to tell us they have been left-behind. We live among them. Perhaps we are one of them. And this is nothing new. The "left-behind," have always been with us. Still, at certain times in history, it becomes stark and sobering. And theologies of glory give us reason to believe it is okay if the "left-behind" suffer. After all, they were not chosen. They brought this on themselves. We tried to make them like us, and they refused. Who are the left-behind?

The poor. The income gap continues to widen in the United States, meaning the middle-class continues to disappear. With automation, AI, and cheap labor in the rest of the world, we will probably see this gap grow even worse. Our economies have left the poor behind even as they prey upon them for their labor and consumption.

The immigrant. Those who have left their nation of birth due to violence, poverty, war, or to seek better lives most certainly feel left-behind. In exile they wait. Unable to return home, and not welcomed abroad, these have already been left-behind.

People of color. Many of us thought we were well past the

racism, even, let's say, of the 1960's. We are not. Racism is alive and well. People of color wake up every day to face a world that seems bent, structured even, to make sure they remember their, "place."

Women. Like racism, many of us also thought we were well past the sexism we grew up with. Even with gains in many areas, we still live in a world that does not see or treat women the same way it does men.

LGBT People. Again, even after making great strides, many still see and treat this group in a way that confirms we will tolerate them, but never accept them. In other parts of the world, they are not even tolerated but persecuted and jailed.

I'm sure I've missed some who also feel left-behind. I'm sure my own privilege, my own blindness, makes it easy for me to miss others, so forgive me. What I would hope fundamentalists-evangelicals could see, is that these people already feel left-behind. They are not worried about missing a future rapture; they are worried about today.

It would be impossible to speak of those left-behind without noting the "election" of Trump and the rapture-believing evangelicals who supported him. We might say his entire life, administration, and purpose have been to cement a "saved" and a "left-behind" mentality into American life. What was already latent- he and his supporters have brought to the surface, to perhaps bring to life the apocalyptic vision of fear and privilege they so clearly believe.

However, from Genesis to Revelation, there is a plumb-line laid down which is clearer and more powerful than any of the proof-texts grabbed here and there to support a dispensational and rapture theology. And that line, that marker, that directional beacon is that the God of the Christian narrative, if nothing else, is the Lord of the left-behind.

Peter Rollins tells illustrative stories to make his points. In his book, *Insurrection,* he tells the following tale:

Just as it was written by those prophets of old, the last days of the Earth overflowed with suffering and pain. In those dark days a huge pale horse rode through the Earth with Death upon its back and Hell in its wake. During this great tribulation, the Earth was scorched with the fires of war, rivers ran red with blood, the soil withheld its fruit, and disease descended like a mist. One by one, all the nations of the Earth were brought to their knees. Far from all the suffering, high up in the heavenly realm, God watched the events unfold with a heavy heart. An ominous silence descended upon Heaven as the angels witnessed the Earth being plunged into darkness and despair. But as this could only continue for so long, at the designated time, God stood upright, breathed deeply, and addressed the angels. "The time has now come for me to separate the sheep from the goats, the healthy wheat from the inedible chaff."

Having spoken these words, God turned to face the world and called forth to the Church with a booming voice, "Rise up and ascend to Heaven, all of you who have sought to escape the horrors of this world by sheltering beneath my wing. Come to me, all who have turned from the suffering world by calling out, 'Lord, Lord,'" and in instant, millions were caught up in the clouds and ascended into the heavenly realm, leaving the suffering world behind them.

Once this great rapture had taken place, God paused for a moment and then addressed the angels, saying, "It is done, I have separated the people born of my spirit from those who have turned from me. It is time now for us to leave this place and take up residence on the Earth, for it is there that we shall find our people, the ones who would forsake Heaven in order to embrace the Earth, the few who would turn away from eternity itself to serve at the feet of a fragile, broken life that passes from existence in but an instant."

And so it was that God and the heavenly host left that place to dwell among those who had rooted themselves upon the

Earth, the ones who had forsaken God for the world and thus who bore the mark of God, the few who had discovered Heaven in the act of forsaking it.[18]

Remember, the Gospel narratives, indeed the entire Christian narrative is one of grand reversals. Thus the "raptured" arrive to find heaven empty. Heaven becomes a purgatory, and the prayer, "Your kingdom come, your will be done, on earth as it is in heaven...," has been fulfilled.

INTRODUCTION TO CHAPTER THREE

If I had to identify one single area that I believed explains most fully the dysfunctional nature of fundamentalism/evangelicalism, it would be their view of the Bible. The holy scriptures are central to the Christian faith. However, we have to be very careful in what we mean by that. The reason the Bible is central to the Christian faith is not because of ink and paper, the arrangement of symbols, but of who it testifies of. It is Jesus who is central to the Christian faith, not the Bible.

This is not to denigrate the Bible; rather, it is to keep the Bible from becoming an idol. I love the Bible. I respect, revere, trust, and hold it in extremely high regard. There is no other book like it in the world and there will never be. I believe the writers of the Bible were divinely inspired. I believe the Holy Spirit guided and influenced the biblical writers. However, it is that which transcends the Bible, Jesus, who is of key importance. If every Bible in the world were to suddenly disappear tomorrow, the Holy Trinity would still exist and be present to us. We must never lose sight of that fact.

Our ultimate trust and faith are in a person, not a book, no matter how sacred. Moreover, our ultimate trust and faith are also not in an interpretation of that person found in our own preconceived biases and backgrounds. Fundamentalists/evangelicals often mistake their reverence and trust in the Bible, for a reverence, and trust in their own interpretations of the Bible. Those are two different things.

The Word of God is Jesus, not a physical book made of paper, leather, and ink. We worship and follow a person, not a book. When we begin to realize we worship not a person, nor even really a book, but our own interpretations of what we think that book teaches, we can begin to see that, in a way, it becomes a worship of self, or one's own construal of others and the world. Making the Bible an idol eventually leads to the rather sobering realization that we have made idols of our own powers of interpretation.

I will address some of this in the following essays, but the usual counter to what I note above is: "But we wouldn't even know Jesus is the Word of God or anything else about him or our faith without the Bible."

The answer to such an objection is this: Learn Christian history. The simple fact is that we would still know all I have mentioned above, even if the Bible never existed. The Bible as we know it, the collection of agreed upon individual books, the canon, did not come into existence until about four hundred years after Christ.

And even before then, it wasn't as if everyone had a copy of the individual books/letters or whole copies of the Hebrew scriptures. It wasn't a literate culture. The majority of people did not read or write. Thus, only those in the priestly classes, the teachers, the elite, the educated, those within powerful subgroups of families and political power had members who could read and write. It was mostly an oral culture, not a written one.

Are we to believe that in those first four centuries, those who followed Christ, those early gatherings, were devoid of teaching and theology? Of course they weren't. They learned that Jesus was the Word of God and all manner of theology well before the Bible was complete or accessible. The Christian faith was robust, active, and vibrant well before the Bible ever makes the scene in any accessible manner, or in a way with which we as moderns are familiar. So, no, everything we know about Christ and the Christian narrative did not depend upon the Bible.

While fundamentalists and evangelicals claim to hold the Bible in high regard, in reality, they do it a great disservice when they use it as something like a textbook, relationship tool, map, newspaper, or encyclopedia. It's not only that they worship their interpretations of the Bible, it's their very view of what the Bible is that becomes toxic and unhelpful.

The Bible is not a science textbook, or a modern textbook at all. It's not a modern marriage or relationship manual. It's not a modern parenting guide. It's not a practical guide to life in general. It's not a code breaking device that allows one to interpret current or future times. And to believe the Bible is any of these things, or to use it this way, is to make the Bible less—to bring it down from its lofty height.

My hope is that this chapter will help us think about the Bible, what it is, and how it should be used, in better ways than what we were probably led to believe by the fundamentalist/evangelical world.

CHAPTER THREE

THE BIBLE

"I JUST GO BY WHAT THE BIBLE SAYS" AND OTHER
RIDICULOUS THINGS PASTORS SAY

If you've spent any time in a fundamentalist or evangelical church, you've probably heard some variation of the following from the pastor or leaders: "I don't preach my opinions, I just preach God's word", or, "I just want to know what the Bible says", or, "I just believe what the Bible says", or, my favorite, "The Bible says it, I believe it, and that settles it."

You get the idea. And even if you haven't heard these exact words, you've likely heard similar sentiments. Often the churches where these ideas and sentiments prevail, will identify themselves as a "Bible Believing Church." The implication here is that there are other Christian churches out there who don't really believe the Bible. I'm not sure what that even means. However, these assertions and the ideas they represent are entirely unhelpful and frankly ridiculous.

The primary idea informing the statements above is that we need to remove ourselves from our Bible reading. We need to stand outside the text, at a distance, so that we don't taint our reading with our own personal subjective opinions and ideas. The Bible just means what it "says" or what is written. Simple. Just open it and read. What's the problem? Wow—where to begin?

First, no one can step outside themselves and interpret any writing from a purely objective space. No such space exists. We are always persons in context. We exist in specific locations, whether culturally, geographically, philosophically, or theologically. We were and are shaped by a myriad of complex influences; many of them we are hardly even aware of. We are the result of a long process of shaping and the influence of others.

We are always "situated." We bring all this to whatever it is we are reading (not just the Bible) and we interpret everything through the lens provided by that shaping. This isn't to say that we are not our own persons, who make up our own minds, but it is to say we are still always doing this from some place, some context, some situated-ness.

If we are aware of this "being situated," then we can read more cautiously and wisely because we are aware of our biases and prejudices. If we are not aware of our always being "situated," however, it can mask those biases and prejudices. Therefore, many Christians read the Bible and what they "hear" only confirms (shocker!) what they already believe. This becomes a reinforcing echo chamber that confirms what we already thought (were taught) and prevents us from ever "hearing" anything in the Bible that would disrupt, deconstruct, or bring under judgment any prejudices or self-serving readings.

What this means is that no one is ever just going by "what the Bible says." When someone tells us the Bible just "says what it says," the natural rejoinder is: "But what does it say?" When someone tells us a passage in the Bible just "means what it means" the natural rejoinder is "But what does it mean?" All those assertions ("I just go by what the Bible says") are nonsense and question-begging.

They are really meant to cut off discussion and prevent disagreement. They are often code for this sentiment: "You are no longer questioning my views or interpretations; you are really questioning God himself and what God has written." How does one respond to that? Those types of statements come from a deep insecurity, fear, and the need to control others. They do not arise out of a real effort to humbly converse, to learn from and engage another person in good faith.

Second, when we are reading, whether the Bible or any other text, we are always interpreting. There is no direct, one-to-one correspondence, between my reading and my assertion regarding what the text means, as if I had some inside line to the very mind of the writer. Unless the writer is literally and physically present to correct us or tell us exactly what they meant, we are always interpreting, which means there are layers to our reading. We are never just letting the Bible speak for itself–if that were the case there would be no need for sermons or teaching. The pastor or priest would simply stand, read the text, and sit down.

Let's be clear about what is really happening when we hear the "I just go by what the Bible says" types of statements. What's really being said is: "I just go by what I have been taught, by what others have thought or written about these passages, and all that is still further interpreted and understood through my own personal, cultural, educational, familial, geographical, social background and history."

Remember, the Bible doesn't "say" anything until someone articulates what they think it is saying. The last time I checked, the Bible did not literally and audibly just start speaking in English to me and I just listened. No, we read it. We are the readers. We must do the hard work of hermeneutics, of inter-preting, which is both an art and a science.

Furthermore, we should always be aware that our interpreta-tions could be wrong. We might completely miss what the author wanted us to hear or understand. Instead of claiming that we are speaking for God or just "going by what the Bible clearly teaches," we need to be humble and admit that we are trying to interpret and understand as best we can—and that it is *us* speaking.

Why is this important? One need only look to the issue of slavery or the way women have been treated historically to point out how wrong the church has at times found itself when it comes to interpreting the Bible. Are there issues in our present day where the church could be making the same interpretive mistakes? No doubt.

Don't be fooled when you hear pastors or church leaders claim, "We are just going by what the Bibles says" or that a passage "just means what it means—what it says." These are not helpful statements or reasons for interpretations. Frankly, I would flee the churches where such ideas and sentiments prevail.

CHRISTIAN: IS YOUR BIBLE AN IDOL?

The Bible is not God, nor do symbols on a page contain God. God is not hiding in the ink or paper molecules/atoms of the Bible. God existed before the Bible. Every time we read or quote a passage of Scripture in an authoritative way, it doesn't mean God is speaking either to us or through us. It simply means we are reading symbols on a page that represent meanings, which we then interpret. Whether or not we truly understand the meaning or purpose of those symbols is something else entirely. It's possible I am idolizing my understanding of those symbols, rather than worshipping (or even interpreting correctly) what they may be pointing toward.

A person could memorize the entire Bible. They could quote a Scripture verse for every problem, argument, or issue at hand. One could study the Bible deeply every day, for a lifetime. One could do all this and never know the God of whom it speaks. One could do this and be a mean, angry, and selfish person. One could do this and never lift a finger for another human being. One could do this and be nothing more than a judgment machine, handing out judgments, opinions, and confident assertions about the world and everyone else.

How do I know this? Because I've experienced it. I know some of these people. I stopped being impressed by people who've memorized a lot of Scripture a long time ago. Why? Because I knew too many of them who were awful people.

Bible knowledge will never substitute for a relationship with the subject of that book. Imagine a woman named Susan. Suppose I have a book about her life. I could read all day long about Susan and memorize much of the information. I might even fall in love with the Susan I read about.

However, it may be the words, the description, the sense I get from the book in my own mind that I'm actually in love with. Not Susan. I've fooled myself. I'm actually in love with my knowledge of Susan—my mental picture of her. I might think to myself, other people know things about her too, but not as much as I do. I love how much I know about her (see the problem?).

However, unless I have actually met Susan and spent time with her and got to know her personally, outside that book, I DO NOT REALLY KNOW SUSAN.

An anticipated response: "But if the Bible is the primary way to know Jesus, if he reveals himself, his thinking, his desires, what he wants from us, in that book, isn't that what is really happening—we are in fact meeting and knowing him through this book?"

First, note how this type of response situates the person contextually in a time (modern) and place (America/the West) where the Bible as we know it is common and readily accessible

—as if our time and location (a short blip on the radar screen of history) was the pinnacle of wisdom on the subject.

The response forgets the first Christians (or the Hebrews before), who did not have what we think of as the complete Bible today. In fact, such would not exist until several centuries after Christ. And guess what, they still knew Jesus, they still knew God. Jesus did not need the presence of a complete Bible before he communicated with his people.

The first Christians had the Hebrew Scriptures and the Apostle's letters in circulation, but this was not a literate culture —most could not read. They came to know Jesus through the spoken words and lives of others, not primarily from a book or Bible as we know it.

As Australian systematic theologian Geoff Thompson has noted:

> "...the fundamentals of Christian faith were already in place in creeds, liturgies and summary statements of faith before the extent of the Christian Scriptures was settled. It was not the Bible which produced Christian belief. Rather, the Bible emerged in the process of clarifying the details of Christian faith. In other words, it was because you believed certain things about Jesus and God that led you to believe certain things about the Bible."[1]

Even in its complete form, regardless of how we think the Bible is inspired or authoritative, it is still not God. The reader, the interpreter is not God. Our thoughts, views, and opinions about what we think the text means, are not God. Our vocal or quoted expressions of the text are not God. Our typing out a verse of Scripture is not God. Our theological frameworks are not God.

Second, such a response completely eschews the ancient mysticism of the Church and the idea that experience, intuition, reason, communal teaching, acting, and the liturgical inhabiting of the faith were also ways in which God as Trinity "spoke" and communicated with the Church, apart from the Bible or written forms.

And just a side note to all this: Fundamentalist Christians (and some evangelicals), when the Church is discussing same-sex attraction, marriage, abortion, the death penalty, gender roles, or any other complicated issue where there is respectful disagreement on both sides, if one thinks merely quoting a Scripture verse somehow settles the matter, then he is incredibly shallow and, frankly, ignorant. If one really thinks the people in those discussions weren't aware of those verses, then I feel sorry for her. It means the person is a child who has wandered into an adult conversation.

Too many fundamentalists (and many evangelicals) make of the Bible, and their understanding of it, an idol. They worship a book and their knowledge of it. Their "relationship" is with a book, rather than with the one of whom it speaks. Christian: Don't make of your Bible an idol—don't be an idol worshipper.

HOW TO READ THE BIBLE

When Christians read the Bible, what is it they want or hope to gain? There are some peripheral things we obviously want. We want to gain a cursory (at least) knowledge of the history, language, culture, the people therein, and the over-arching story the Bible tells. These are basic desires most of us bring to our Bible reading.

However, I don't think this gets to what we really desire. I think what most of us genuinely want is to hear from God. We want God to speak to us through the Bible. Whether it is a word personally to us regarding something in our lives known only to us, or whether it is to address issues outside our personal lives, we desire to hear God speak through the Bible, in the here-and-now.

Most of us—God I hope so—know I am not talking about a literal, audible voice, but something deep in our spirits and souls, something that comes to us beyond our own thoughts or psychology. If you are someone who doesn't believe this can happen, then read no further. Most Christians, however, do believe this is possible. And it is, I think, what they truly desire when reading the Bible. How is this possible then?

Before addressing that question, there are two misunder-standings many Christians bring to Bible reading that prevents the very thing they desire. This is especially true if one comes out of the fundamentalist/evangelical world. The first misunder-standing is that the amount of Bible reading one does, memo-rization, knowing chapter and verse, and actual time spent reading the Bible, will automatically lead to understanding the Bible better and hearing from God. I don't believe that is true.

The reasons are this: First, the figure we know as the "devil," probably knows more of the Bible word-for-word, than any of us or any biblical scholar, past or present. Second, the pharisees, scribes, and priests knew the "Bible" of Jesus's time extremely well. And yet, many of them missed Jesus! With all that, "Bible" knowledge, Jesus still called some of them, "sons of hell."[2] Jesus's harshest words were reserved for the "biblical" scholars and teachers of his day, not tax collectors or prostitutes.

Folks: *There has to be a lesson in there somewhere.*

The second misunderstanding is that understanding the Bible correctly and hearing from God starts with the simple act of reading the Bible. I don't believe this is true either. As modern Christians we often forget that for the first several centuries of the church, Christians, including those who were priests/pastors and leaders, did not have an individual Bible (as we know it today) to read. The very few educated and literate leaders had, at most, a single copy of the Hebrew Scriptures

(Old Testament) and maybe a copy of a letter or two circulating from some of the apostles. And yet, these people still heard from God.

Those early Christians were steeped in prayer, spiritual disciplines, community, and loving action. They had an oral tradition of the words of Jesus and the memories of the lived lives of the saints and martyrs before them. They had stories from the Hebrew Scriptures passed on orally. What they did not have, was their own personal Bible under their arm they could read each day—or whenever they wanted. The great majority were not even literate. It was an oral culture, not a reading culture. This went on for centuries. And yet, these people still heard from God.

Putting those two misunderstandings aside, how do we read the Bible? How do we hear from God in his word? How do we interpret and understand the Bible? My own answers to those questions are somewhat paradoxical. I would address those questions, first, by saying we don't start with the Bible. Something has to happen before we even open the Bible.

First, we need a community. A caveat: Clearly there are examples of people, whether in a hotel room by themselves, or in a prison cell, who simply opened a Bible and started reading and experienced something spiritually significant. There is no method or approach that covers everyone's experience or that could possibly include every possible situation where the Spirit of God could speak.

Putting that caveat aside, before we open our Bibles we need to be catechized or taught. We need to read the Bible in community. And by community, I mean both presently and with the community from ages past. We need to hear the voices of those outside our own time and echo chamber.

Why? Because our reading isn't a matter of our personal, individualistic take on, "what it means to me," without any understanding or awareness of what the community of readers have thought it (whatever passage we are reading) meant over time. This isn't to say we cannot read the Bible by ourselves, whether in private devotion or study. However, whatever comes of such times should always be brought back into the community of Christian learning and balanced against the greater whole.

Finally, here, I believe, is the key—the one thing needed—to understanding the Bible, interpreting it correctly, and being able to "hear" God speak: Love. I submit that without love, toward God and neighbor, we cannot truly understand the Bible nor hear from God through the written word, no matter our technical mastery of the literature.

We may have a very scholarly and educated grasp of the Bible, we may have read the Bible many times over, but without love, I don't honestly believe those other things (although important) ultimately matter. Here is the connection to my first point: Our community should be forming us through the spiritual disciplines, through the liturgy, prayer, and service to become people who love—especially their enemies.

God is love (early Christians were taught this before the Bible existed as we know it). Love is the interpretive key. With it, all scriptural doors are open to us. God speaks to those who love, not to those who "understand all mysteries and all knowledge..." (1 Cor 13:2).

I take nothing away from an educated and scholarly reading of the Bible. There are wonderful hermeneutical tools out there to help us. We should avail ourselves of all those tools. Read well and often. Spend time in conversation with theologians and philosophers. Think. Reflect. Do the hard-intellectual work required on your part.

But, ultimately, without love, all those efforts and knowledge become simple excavating tools, good only for the digging up of dead bodies and ancient ruins. Love is what allows the Bible to become a living, breathing, present-moment-voice to us. Love is also what allows us to correctly interpret and apply the Bible in our lives. Otherwise, it can be (and has been) used to justify all manner of evil.

My two cents: Read in community—meaning communities both past and present. Read from a life of love toward God and neighbor. This is, I believe, how to read, understand, and interpret the Bible, so that we put ourselves in a place where we can, "hear" from God.

After all, isn't that what we truly desire?

I WANT "CHAPTER AND VERSE"

Something evangelicals and fundamentalists pride themselves on is their reliance upon the Bible as the last word in anything and everything. If there is an assertion, a teaching, an opinion, some way of thinking or viewing a situation, the pious fundamentalist/evangelical wants "chapter and verse" to back it up or support whatever has been asserted.

Obviously for Christians, the Bible is a special collection of writings. Christians believe these writings to be of divine origin, blessed, and more than the thoughts and intentions of human writers alone. These writings make up the narrative of God's working from the beginning of creation to the final judgment and summing up of all things.

However, there are a number of problems with the evangelical sensibility that comes with the "chapter and verse" mentality.

First, the Bible, while important, is only one part of God's revelation. In theology, we speak of general revelation and special revelation. General revelation is the physical/material creation. God speaks through what has been made. If we listen to the created order with the proper attitude (love) and posture (humility), we can hear God speak. While the Bible is considered special revelation, it is not the only voice God has. A "chapter and verse" sensibility can too often lead us to forget the importance of general revelation.

Second, there is the revelation of the incarnation (God became flesh—Jesus—in history). While we might surmise that we could only know this through information from the Bible, such is not true. Even if there had never been a Bible as we know it now, the incarnation would still have happened, and its truth would have been carried down by oral tradition and changed lives. We need to remember that for the first four centuries after Christ, we did not have the Bible as we know it. During that same time, the followers of Jesus "turned the world upside down,"[3] and literally changed the course of Western Civilization.

Before the Bible as we know it today was compiled, Christians had teachers (who had lived with Jesus for three years), an oral tradition from those teachers, some of the letters of the New Testament in circulation (but not each and every person had access to their own copy), and the Jewish Scriptures (Old or First Testament). Most importantly, they had the Holy Spirit to lead and teach them. A "chapter and verse" type of mentality probably wasn't a very broad or prevalent notion in the Church body of those first few centuries—because it wouldn't have made sense in their context or circumstances.

My point however is that not having the Bible as we do now, or the same access we do, did not seem to prevent them from accomplishing far more than many of the generations, who had both, that came after. Something to ponder.

Third, a "chapter and verse" mentality can be very deceptive. It was my experience that what people meant when they wanted chapter and verse, was: As to what this person's asserting—is it correct theology, i.e., my theology, what I have been taught, and what I have decided the Bible teaches as to this subject or question?

In other words, it wasn't really a request to see what Scripture the person could cite to support their assertion, opinion, or thought. It was more of a sentiment along these lines: I don't think the Bible supports what you are suggesting and by that, I mean I don't think it comports with my theology or understanding of what the Bible teaches.

Here is the deception, however. What the person often truly believes is that we are not simply disagreeing about interpretation, theology, or understanding, but we are disagreeing with the Bible itself, and therefore, God. The, "I want chapter and verse," then, is a sort of ruse. It can often be an authoritarian appeal, to position the other person into a place where we can claim that the disagreement isn't with us, but with God. It's a nice bait and switch.

I'm all for backing up one's significant claims with Scripture, but only if we mean our take, our interpretation, and our (limited) understanding of those Scriptures. Further, that we could be wrong, and that there are other sources of information we should also consider. Since Christians believe all truth is God's truth, we should consider then what we can learn from all sorts of different traditions, sciences, philosophies, cultures, historical timeframes, etc.

We should also consider and listen to the arts. Music, poetry, literature, painting, and creative artistic expression in all forms can speak to us—meaning the Spirit can speak through them to us. The Wisdom of God is at work in the creative arts because God was the first poet and creator. The God of the Christian narrative is the first and greatest artist and the Spirit moves in such efforts.

We should also consider the Christian (Holy) tradition, our best theologians, both current and historical. We should consider the oral traditions and how interpretations have changed over the centuries. All these sources and avenues should be considered.

The "chapter and verse" mentality is too limited and truncated. It provides a narrow gaze, rather than a wide, open, and expanded gaze, which clearly is the better way in which to view anything. It is not only a better, more accurate way to look at things, but is the wiser course as well.

Christians need to understand they can learn from others, yes, even the "unsaved" or those who do not claim to be Christians.

This is true for all of us, whether atheist, religious, agnostic, or what have you—not just Christians. We can learn from those we disagree with or who have fundamentally different worldviews. They may still have something important to say (all are image bearers of God) to us if we have the humility to listen. This doesn't mean we have to agree with their core beliefs, but we have to be open to the possibility the Spirit could be speaking through sources other than those we would normally expect—isn't that what Israel missed?

I write of course from a Christian perspective (thus the belief all people are image bearers of God). However, if one doesn't believe in "spirit" or "god" then accept the fact the other person could be speaking from a knowledge, a wisdom, experience, or insight you do not yet possess. Which is all to say, any one of us could be wrong and even though we might hold our beliefs with confidence, we should hold even our deepest beliefs with a corollary humility.

After all, isn't that the same grace, humility, and openness we hope others will extend to us when we are trying to speak our truth?

THE IRRELEVANCY OF INERRANCY

The Maginot Line[4] was a series of fortifications built by the French after World War I. Its purpose was to prevent or slow down another attack and invasion by Germany. We all know how that turned out. Rather than come directly at these fortifications, which probably were impregnable and almost indestructible, the Germans simply went around them.

The Maginot Line was constructed to fight the last war, to address past strategies and threats. I think the belief in an inerrant Bible[5] is much like a Maginot Line. It was something constructed by those who felt under threat, who felt their world was being invaded by hostile actors. And as with the historical Line, it has been bypassed. And the conversation has advanced far past whatever ground it was supposed to hold or protect.

I am not bothered much by its failure. I remember when the belief in inerrancy was (and sometimes still is) weaponized and used more as a blunt object than it was for anything constructive.[6] I saw it used to target, put down, fire, quiet, or shun people. In my experience, it has left a lot of damage in its wake. I shed no tears over its diminishing pertinence or relevance.

Inerrancy is mostly irrelevant due to the modern/postmodern divide. Inerrancy was a way of defending the authority of scripture, when we all thought we had to play by the rules of modernity. It was an unconscious acceptance of the modern as the reigning narrative. Those most invested in inerrancy never seemed to notice their capitulation to the modern rationalist mindset, even mistaking it for "historic" or "ancient" Christian understandings.

Merold Westphal gets to much of this in his wonderful little book entitled, *Whose Community? Which Interpretation?* with the subtitle of *Philosophical Hermeneutics for the Church*.[7] In the very first chapter he speaks of naïve realism[8] and truth as correspondence.[9] These are two of the hallmarks of modernity. They both touch on epistemology and hermeneutics.

When we consider the Chicago Statement[10] and other articulations of inerrancy, we can see the underlying commitment to both these hallmarks. Bound up in naïve realism is the idea of "common sense." An object or a text is no more than it appears to be—what does our "common sense" tell us about it? This should allow us all to "see" or interpret this object or text the same. Westphal writes:

"Common sense...does claim to 'just see' its objects, free of bias, prejudice, and presuppositions (at least sometimes). We can call this 'just seeing' intuition. When the naïve-realist view of knowledge and understanding is applied to reading texts, such as the Bible, it becomes the claim that we can 'just see' what the text means, that intuition can and should be all we need. In other words, 'no interpretation needed.' The object, in this case the meaning of the text, presents itself clearly and directly to my reading. To interpret would be to interject some subjective bias or prejudice (pre-judgment) into the process. Thus the response, 'Well, that might be your interpretation, but my Bible clearly says...' In other words, 'You interpret (and thereby misunderstand), but I intuit, seeing directly, clearly, and without distortion.'"[11]

Naïve realism, Westphal goes on to note, is maintained to preserve truth as correspondence. These are complex terms and I would recommend one research them thoroughly; a single chapter cannot do either justice. A source like the *Stanford Encyclopedia of Philosophy* is a good place to start. However, one should not claim inerrancy or spend much time defending it unless one is familiar with these terms (naïve realism, realism in general, and truth as correspondence) and the arguments for and against.

Westphal asks the critical question: "Why seek to avoid interpretation?" And he suggests one reason that, out of a generosity of spirit I think we should dismiss:

"Let us turn to the question of motivation. Why would anyone want to hold to a hermeneutical version of naïve realism? Let us dismiss (but not too quickly) the suspicion that this view is attractive because it makes it easy to say: 'I am (we are) right, and all who disagree are wrong...'"[12]

I love the qualifier we should not dismiss the reason "too

quickly." One has to wonder if inerrancy isn't so much about protecting and defending the Bible (which needs protecting about as much as a lion might against a mouse), as it is protecting and defending personal or tribal interpretations. What we too often want is a way to defend our personal interpretations of the Bible, in a way where we bring God in on our side. What an ally, right? Is this the role inerrancy plays?

The Chicago Statement was put out in 1978. The conversation regarding the post-modern (which is not the bogey-man many conservatives make it out to be[13]) and how it applies to hermeneutics; the related issues raised by Heidegger, Gadamer, Ricoeur, as treated by many scholars; the more recent work of many evangelicals (Clark Pinnock, Peter Enns, Kenton Sparks, Kevin Vanhoozer, Andrew McGowan, Stanley Grenz—and more —all have moved the conversation well past 1978).

Inerrancy is just one more area where fundamentalists and many evangelicals are simply too modern. N.T. Wright sums up the problem nicely:

> "My book on scripture's authority, *Scripture and the Authority of God*, makes clear where I stand. I take the whole of scripture utterly seriously, and I regret that many who call themselves "inerrantists" manage to avoid the real challenge at its heart, that is, Jesus' announcing that in and through his work God really was 'becoming king' over the world in a whole new way. So I don't call myself an "inerrantist" (a) because that word means what it means within a modernist rationalism, which I reject and (b) because it seems to me to have failed in delivering a full-blooded reading and living of what the Bible actually says. It may have had a limited usefulness as a label against certain types of 'modernist' denial, but it buys into at least half of the rationalist worldview which was the real problem all along."[14]

All this and more has made inerrancy, in my view, irrelevant to current theological and philosophical conversations regarding hermeneutics and epistemology. In my opinion, inerrancy should be seen, like the Maginot Line, as a historical footnote bearing witness to the futility of building defensive constructs based upon the last war and even, in this case, using the same philosophical building materials as the very opponents they feared.

EVANGELICALS ARE ATTRACTED TO CONSPIRACY THEORIES—WHY?

Many voices from across the evangelical spectrum have all noted the same problem, which is that too many evangelicals in the pews are prone to believe and echo conspiracy theories.[15]

However, while these critics, to their credit, note the problem—there don't seem to be many theories as to why evangelicals do this. They point out the harm it does, but, again, not why the problem exists. Few seem to wonder why there is this bent, this readiness to believe the preposterous, to begin with. What are its origins?

Perhaps one of the problems these Protestant/evangelical critics miss is their own theology and history, which I think plays a key role in the very problem noted. While they may not hold to some of the beliefs or understandings I will address shortly, they belong to a tradition where these beliefs have had a significant and foundational influence on evangelicals in the pews (chairs now).

As an aside, growing up in evangelicalism as a Southern Baptist, and looking back now, I would suggest that many who call themselves evangelical are in reality fundamentalists. That was my experience, although it is purely anecdotal. Regardless, in truth, there is not much separation between the two when it comes to core theology. It's mostly a difference of sensibility, education, and culture. The problem, in my view, is that the core theology still contains the same problems for either. Thus, my critique is of both.

Here are some of the reasons I believe too many evangelicals/fundamentalists (E/Fs) are prone to believing conspiracy theories:

First, their view of the Bible. If the Bible is held to be true in the same way a science or mathematics textbook is "true," then all sorts of folly is sure to follow. Such a view opens the door to doubting acknowledged experts, the academy, proven authorities, and accepted bodies of knowledge, if they disagree with or don't support this groups' interpretation of the Bible, whatever the subject matter. This allows E/Fs to dismiss or discount information they think contradicts the Bible (or their interpretation thereof). This in turn creates an openness to a belief in conspiracy theories, often the alternative explanation for whatever the issue might be.

Second, their eschatology or understanding of the End Times. Any E/F growing up in the 70s, 80s, and even 90s can tell stories about pastors and leaders taking the book of Revelation and applying it to current world events. How they applied it, though, is key. The assumption was always that no matter what was occurring, however mundane or banal, only they knew its "true" meaning, because they understood the book of Revelation. Thus, for example, any new technology pertinent to commerce was really about getting people to accept the Mark of the Beast (666), and any new helicopter the Israelis developed was really what the book of Revelation (9:7) described as locusts. This type of eschatology, it turns out, is a gateway to believing conspiracy theories and frankly, all sorts of nonsense.

Finally, their past pastors, theologians, and leaders. For decades, E/Fs have followed and listen to a parade of people spouting conspiracy theories. Indeed, many were quite influential and revered. E/Fs bought their books, went to their conferences, and supported their ministries. From Hal Lindsey, to Tim Lahaye, to Pat Robertson and many others, the E/F landscape is strewn with famous figures spewing conspiracy theories. These theories ranged from the identity of the anti-Christ, to the fear of Freemasons, the Rothschilds, the Illuminati, and a one-world-government. Long before the internet, so-called "fake news," and QAnon, E/Fs were already believing in, and echoing, conspiracy theories. They are a ready-made audience for our present moment and current conspiracy theories.

These three reasons are hardly exhaustive. There are certainly others. For instance, one could cite the problems noted by evangelical historian Mark Noll.[16] Additionally, a significant factor is the reliance upon conspiracy minded "news" platforms such as Fox News, One America News (OAN), Newsmax, YouTube, Right-Wing Talk Radio, and a myriad of internet black holes of unmitigated ignorance and misinformation.

However, notice a common thread through my three reasons? The second and third point back to the first.

As long as E/Fs continue to understand the Bible the way they do, this gullibility and lack of discernment as to conspiracy theories will probably continue. An understanding of the Bible as literal truth, or as something we should view like a modern science textbook, encyclopedia, tends to form people prone to conspiracy theories. Why? Because the Bible is not that type of literature. If read and understood that way, it can easily lead to conspiratorial understandings due to the confusion of metaphor and the poetic with the literal. It's another reason E/Fs tend to be receptive to, and easily manipulated by, television preachers and political leaders; witness our current moment!

Here is what I believe these evangelical critics are missing as they rightfully and courageously address this problem in their own camp: A key factor is the underlying theology, specifically a view of the Bible, and how E/Fs understand inspiration, authority, and beliefs like "Scripture alone." Until they are willing to address those issues, the problem is sure to continue, as it has now, for decades.

OPEN BIBLES—OPEN MINDS

Something I found growing up in the fundamentalist-evangelical world was that having a closed mind was almost championed as a good thing. The more one knew about Scripture and the less one knew about "secular" literature, science, movies, music, popular culture, and philosophy, the more "spiritual" one was considered to be. Ignorance of things outside the Bible was often worn as a badge of honor.

Looking back, I think, how very sad. Also, how very contrary to the Christian faith and narrative. An open Bible should lead to an open mind. An open Bible should lead to an ever expanding and growing realization that we know very little. As we learn about the deep things of God and creation, the more curious we should become. After all, creation/existence is a big thing. The moment we think we know all we need to know, about anything, we reveal a disturbing lack of curiosity and a fairly shallow mentality.

I'm amazed at the people who because of their supposed Bible knowledge, tell us they don't need to really delve deeply into other areas like science, political science, philosophy, social science, or all the other areas of knowledge. Holding up their Bible, they boldly claim all they need to know is contained in its pages. They then go on to pontificate about subjects they have very little knowledge of (admittedly, proudly), beyond popular opinion, sheer prejudice, or stereotypes. They become the guy at the end of the bar blathering on about his latest conspiracy theory, which he's "researched" deeply on the internet. Got it.

They view experts and academics with suspicion; and also news stories that don't confirm or support what they already believe—which explains many of the anti-maskers. They are sure the fact they have memorized large portions of Scripture qualifies them to summarily dismiss people who have spent much of their lives studying, writing, publishing, and speaking in areas where they are widely recognized as experts or scholars. But what are years of learning at the highest levels, recognized learning, when one can just memorize portions of the Bible or follow some guy on the internet?

I'm stating nothing new or novel. We have supposed intelligent evangelicals calling widely recognized facts "fake news." Fake? No, it's just news they don't like—news that doesn't support the world they've constructed in their closed universe. Or we have appeals to the "common sense" of conventional "wisdom" in whatever area.

Here is a good example:

> Think about it. Why have Americans been able to do more to help people in need around the world than any other country in history? It's because of free enterprise, freedom, ingenuity, entrepreneurism and wealth. A poor person never gave anyone a job. A poor person never gave anybody charity, not of any real volume. It's just common sense to me.[17]

To the contrary, we read:

> Jesus looked up and saw the rich putting their gifts into the offering box, and he saw a poor widow put in two small copper coins. And he said, 'Truly, I tell you, this poor widow has put in more than all of them. For they all contributed out of their abundance, but she out of her poverty put in all she had to live on.'[18]

So much for "common sense." Falwell, Jr. probably believes because of his upbringing and history, that he knows the Bible well. But statements like his (and recent events—Google it) prove the opposite. Somewhere along the line his supposed Bible "knowledge" became a closed room, a dead end, something much smaller than the wide expanse of creation and what creation can tell us. Or it became a secular understanding covered with a religious veneer, simply assumed to be true, even "biblical."

Closed quarters, where all one can see is walls, where everything in the room is familiar, leads to the illusion that this is all there is, that we "know" it all. It becomes a very small world. And yet, a look out the window, if any still remain, reveals such not to be true at all. To wish to remain in ignorance, to even consider it a virtue, is shameful. It's certainly not the sign of a mature Christian.

Truly knowing the Bible, which really means knowing its author, should always lead to an open mind, a mind that recognizes how little it really knows. It should lead to a mind that realizes all of existence (including the poor) has something to teach us (Psalm 19). Further, such knowledge will often come from sources and places well outside our culture, ethnic group, religious tradition, education level, historical time-frame, or familiar worldview.

In Daniel we read: "As for these four youths, God gave them learning and skill in all literature and wisdom…"[19]

Notice this is something God gave, and it was in "all" literature and wisdom, not just in what these young men were used to, already knew, or brought up with.

As Christians, we believe all truth is God's truth. But not everything we believe, or think, or were taught, or interpreted, or heard somewhere once from our favorite preacher is true. Too often what we think is "common sense" is nonsense we just assume is true. A closed and uncurious mind is nothing to be proud of.

Open Bibles should lead to open minds, not the opposite.

THE "SUFFICIENCY OF SCRIPTURE" SLOGAN IS A DODGE

What do Protestants in general, specifically fundamental-
ists/evangelicals, mean when they speak of *the sufficiency of Scripture*. Here, in a general way, is a fairly good take on what they
mean. This writer from the Gospel Coalition[20] defines the idea
this way:

"Scripture is sufficient in that it is the only inspired,
inerrant, and therefore final authority for Christians for faith
and godliness, with all other authorities being subservient to
Scripture."

The writer goes on to note that this doesn't mean we should
never avail ourselves of extra-biblical sources. He writes:

Does sufficiency mean all extra-biblical resources should be
eliminated? No. To say it does is to confuse sola scriptura with
nuda scriptura. Remember, sola scriptura does not preclude
other authorities in the church (such as creeds, councils, church
leaders, theologians, traditions, etc.). Rather, it is to say Scripture alone is our inspired, inerrant, and therefore final authority.
While there may be many important authorities, they are all
subservient to Scripture, which alone is God-breathed and
without error, fully trustworthy and sufficient for faith and practice. Scripture alone is our magisterial authority; all other
authorities are ministerial.

The writer also goes into the historical circumstances of
where this understanding (*sola scriptura*) came from—it being a
part of the Reformation's break with Rome in general. The
Catholic and Eastern Orthodox streams of thought take a high
view of tradition and the papal or conciliar decisions regarding
doctrine and practice. However, those traditions also believe
there is no conflict between those and scripture. Protestants
disagree, but that is another matter.

Here, in my view, is the problem with the idea or assertion of the sufficiency of scripture: It's a dodge—in reality it doesn't mean anything. It operates more as a slogan than anything substantive. What does it dodge? The matter of interpretation and the matter of how interpretation is never done in a vacuum. For instance, the writer asserts this:

As seen in these confessional statements, sufficiency distinguishes the Protestant evangelical, who turns to Scripture as that which contains all that is necessary for salvation and godliness.

What is really being asserted here though? It isn't that we turn to the Bible as that "which contains all that is necessary..." We turn to our interpretations of what the Bible contains—interpretations already formed by a presupposition of sufficiency understood in a specific and historical context.

Even Catholics and Eastern Orthodox would assert that the Bible contains all that is necessary for salvation and godliness. However, they would also add, and correctly so, that such has to be interpreted correctly, and what helps us do that is tradition and the teaching authorities in those traditions.

A clear tell though comes here: "Nonetheless, we should naturally worry if any extrabiblical source claims superiority to scriptural truth or poses itself in opposition to biblical Christianity."

I hate to break this to the writer, but inanimate extrabiblical sources don't claim anything. And neither does the Bible. Only people make claims. I've never placed my ear real close to the Bible and heard it claim anything. Science, history, philosophy, social science, astronomy, geology, archeology, or any other area of inquiry one wants to name do not make claims of superiority or opposition to anything. People do.

And people make those claims depending upon how they

interpret the information, the facts, and the evidence provided by any source of information, biblical or otherwise. The way they interpret said information is through the philosophical presuppositions they bring to bear. All information/knowledge is *interpreted* information and knowledge. Further, it is all done in a context of a myriad of other factors and influences.

Does that mean we can have our own "facts" or that there are "alternative" facts? No. But it does mean that facts/information/evidence can be viewed differently, from different perspectives, and lead to more than one reasonable conclusion. If one doesn't believe this, simply delve into the history of science or any area of inquiry.

But I digress. Back to the point, when fundamentalists/evangelicals tell us they are worried about an extrabiblical source becoming a superior or greater authority than the Bible, what they really mean is they fear another source may question or even possibly demonstrate that their interpretation of the Bible is wrong. Some good examples would be the belief in a 6000-year-old earth or pre-Civil War views of slavery.

It's clearly difficult for fundamentalists/evangelicals to see the possibility that only their interpretation might be wrong or in question and not the Bible's content or authority. This just reveals how much they have mixed up all these aspects to begin with. Look, the Bible may be sufficient in many things, but that doesn't mean our interpretation or understanding of the Bible is —and that's the true issue.

INTRODUCTION TO CHAPTER FOUR

In my heart and mind, I had slowly been leaving the fundamentalist/evangelical world since about 2005 or so. However, I was still, even then, a leader in an evangelical (Southern Baptist) church. I was an elder, a small group leader, and part of our worship team. In fact, I had led this church as pastor from 2000 to 2005. After five years, I decided to step out of that role (long story—but mostly it had to do with spending time with my Dad before he passed away) and let someone else lead while I became part of the leadership team.

I knew this couldn't continue long since my views were becoming drastically different than the views of our church and those around me. I had confided all this to the person who had taken my place as lead pastor and he was actually very sympathetic and understanding. While he disagreed with me on many issues, he still wanted me to remain in the roles I was then filling. I had many wonderful friendships there and loved these people greatly, so it was easy for me to stay and just overlook the other differences.

People have asked me if there was one moment or single event that finally caused my break with the fundamentalist/evangelical world. My answer is usually "yes" and "no." What I mean is that I knew deep in my heart that once I left the current church I was in, I would never again become a member of another fundamentalist/evangelical church gathering. I knew at that point I would seek out more progressive fellowships and gatherings and ones that were liturgical and better connected to the ancient church. It was only a matter of time, but it could wait until I left that church where I had so many wonderful friendships and memories.

However, that all changed in 2016. I then experienced the most disappointing moment in my life with regard to white fundamentalists/evangelicals—in other words, *my people*. When I learned that 81% of white evangelicals voted for Trump, my heart sank. This was unbelievable. How in the world did a group of people, who for decades, had told us principles and character were more important than policy, labels, or political views, vote for a man who had neither?

These people had railed against Bill Clinton for his indiscretions while president and even before. They supported his being impeached. But then, power was dangled before them like a hypnotist's watch. Here was a man (Trump) whose entire life up to that point had been marked by ignorance, adultery, failed marriages, womanizing, paying off porn stars, bankruptcies, fraud, stiffing vendors and contractors, love of money and power, lawsuits, being a pathological liar and a narcissist, hardly what anyone would consider wise or intelligent. He was certainly not a religious person, church going, or someone familiar with the Bible.

He was the very opposite of everything evangelicals had ever said was important, in a person running for the highest office in the land. They threw it all out the window simply because they had been radicalized by Fox News to hate Hillary Clinton (an actual church going—Methodist—Christian) and, I believe, because she was a woman. She was certainly more intelligent, more experienced, more decent, and more Christian than Trump —sorry, those are just empirical facts. The sort of facts only ideology, propaganda, and hatred could blind one to.

Was she perfect? Of course not, no one is. Let's put that aside. Fundamentalists/evangelicals could have voted third party or wrote in someone else. They had options.

But because Trump, who had been *pro-choice his entire life* up until deciding to run for president, changed and said he was now "pro-life," that was the icing on the cake for white evangelicals. Along with their *programmed* hatred for Hillary and their *built-in sexist views* toward women in leadership, this one policy view made them now comfortable enough to throw whatever principles they had left, out the window.

The stench from that sort of hypocrisy was too much for me to bear. If there was a final straw in my leaving that world, it was the election of Trump and the support he received from the very people I thought knew better. If one's theology, political philosophy, cultural and historical awareness was that shallow and weak, then it truly confirmed my worst fears about the tradition of my childhood and young adulthood. Conversely, to look at it positively, it also gave me a clear conscience and a go-ahead to finally leave that world.

It was shortly after the election that I asked our lead pastor to have dinner with me. That would have been sometime in November or early December. I told him the last Sunday of December would be my last Sunday as a member and leader of that fellowship. I explained my reasons. To begin with, he was not really a political person or someone who followed politics very closely. He seemed to be unaware of or indifferent to the catastrophe of the moment, of the failing of our tradition in the political realm. I wasn't sure what was worse, the indifference and unawareness (the category he seemed to fall into, regardless of who he voted for), or the active, cogent, and purposeful support of someone as loathsome as Trump. At that point, it didn't matter.

I was raised up in a world that saw America as chosen by God, another Israel, a nation that was special. It was a "Christian" nation (tell that to the native Americans or the descendants of slaves). It's political arrangements, even its founding documents, were almost of divine origin in a sense. Its founding fathers were Christians, clearly establishing a Christian nation (never mind that wall of separation business). To love God was to also love America and it was our "manifest destiny" to expand and lead (rule) the world as more of a theocracy than a republic or democracy.

That is what I was taught or is what I was led to believe by some of the best-known fundamentalists/evangelicals of the 1970s and 80s. However, it was all nonsense. It was historically, politically, philosophically, and theologically pure horse feces. It was inaccurate in almost every way conceivable. It was a myth. More importantly, it was a dangerous myth. It's the sort of myth that leads to insurrection, violence, death, and even possibly civil war. It's a myth of power, division, and suspicion of the "other."

These next set of essays speak to this whole area and it may be the most important section of the entire book given our present moment. As I write this it is 2021 and we are still not out of the woods yet as to Trump, a radicalized GOP, white supremacy, nationalism, and the future of our republic. Everything, our political arrangements, what we think of as "America," and American culture—is hanging in the balance. Please read the next chapter prayerfully and carefully.

CHAPTER FOUR
THE POLITICAL-CULTURAL

CHRISTIAN: YOU ARE UPSET ABOUT THE WRONG THINGS

Sociologist Tony Campolo has been known, when speaking to Christian audiences, to begin by saying something like this:

> I have three things I'd like to say today. First, while you were sleeping last night, 30,000 kids died of starvation or diseases related to malnutrition. Second, most of you don't give a shit. What's worse is that you're more upset with the fact I just said "shit" than you are that 30,000 kids died last night.

When citing this, I have had people prove his very point by responding with something to the effect of, "Yeah, I get it, but I still wish he would make his point some other way..." Well, that is his point. Yes, he is making the point we should care and do something about starving children, but his greater point is that we (Christians) get upset over the wrong things. Our moral sense of outrage is often misdirected. We are offended by the wrong things.

That we first notice the offensive language before we really register the fact children are dying, tells us all we need to know. Any focus on a crude term and not on his greater point that children are dying of starvation or malnutrition and that we might be complicit proves his very point. If there was a tiny gasp from the crowd at that word or an awkward silence—such reactions were misdirected. These people were upset about the wrong thing.

The legalistic, simplistic, and shallow world of fundamentalism (and even many aspects of evangelicalism) breeds some rather odd triggers for what it is we are supposed to get upset about. Here are just a few:

If we become upset when hearing that gay marriage is legal or that a transgender person may use the same public restroom as us, but we are less upset regarding the hate, violence, and discrimination directed toward such people, often leading to suicide...: *We are upset about the wrong things.*

If we become upset when people use the greeting "Happy Holidays" instead of "Merry Christmas," but we are less upset at the wasteful use of resources during this season and the rampant shallow consumerism while many live in poverty...: *We are upset about the wrong things.*

If we become upset when the government uses its power to make corporations protect their workers and protect the environment, but we are less upset when those workers are exploited, injured, or the environment is critically harmed...: *We are upset about the wrong things.*

If we become upset at the grocery store when we see someone pay for their food with vouchers or food stamps, but we are less upset with the institutional and cultural structures that often create the very need for such help...: *We are upset about the wrong things.*

If we become upset when we see people smoking cigarettes or drinking alcohol, but we are less upset when we see people over-eating, knowing the health effects of such, or wasting food, knowing that people go to bed hungry every night...: *We are upset about the wrong things.* (Please note: this example has nothing to do with fat shaming or singling out people who struggle with weight issues—it speaks to gluttony—which is a sin)

If we become upset when Hollywood puts out movies that contain coarse language or nudity, but we are less upset with the excessive, sadistic, and pornographic displays of violence, murders, gore, and bloodletting in war movies, action movies, or even movies like *The Passion of the Christ*...: We are upset about the wrong things.

If we become upset when the government tries to pass reasonable gun restriction laws, but we are less upset with the amount of accidental firearm-related deaths among children and the general level of gun violence in America...: *We are upset about the wrong things.*

If we become upset when we feel the government is restricting our religious liberties, but we are less upset or even applaud the restriction of the religious liberties of others...: *We are upset about the wrong things.*

If we become upset when someone commits adultery or at the sexual lapses of others, but we are less upset at the people who gather around to stone them, or gather around to throw insults, or gossip, or shun them, or shame them, or pass laws to single them out...: *We are upset about the wrong things.*

If we get upset over an NFL player kneeling during the National Anthem, the timing and manner of protest, but not over what is being protested, the treatment and killing of unarmed Black men...: *We are upset about the wrong things.*

If we get upset over a Civil War monument being torn down, monuments that many see as celebrating treason and slavery, if the destruction of stone is more upsetting to us than the destruction of the lives those monuments bear witness to…: *We are upset over the wrong things.*

One could go on and on.

Let me address the anticipated response: "Can't we be upset with both?" Yes, of course (rightly or wrongly). The point, however, is that those aspects pale in significance when placed alongside the deeper and much more important moral failing noted—the failing that should really upset us. It would be like someone telling Jesus, just before he overturned the money-changer's tables and grabbed a whip, how upset they were at the price of doves that year. It isn't a false dichotomy. It's a problem of scale. To respond in such a way only proves the very point.

I am reminded of a scene in the movie *Life is Beautiful*[1] where we see Guido (Roberto Benigni) so happy to think that his old friend, the Nazi doctor, will help him after the doctor recognizes him and makes his life easier inside the death camp. The doctor remembers how clever his friend was, and how he could solve difficult riddles.

We begin to think the doctor realizes the moral wrongness of the death camp. Maybe he will try and save Guido and his family. But no, we finally realize, as does Guido, that the doctor simply wanted help solving a riddle. He doesn't see Guido or the suffering. That doesn't upset him. What upsets him is not finding the answer to something as insignificant as a riddle. He even says he can't sleep at night because of it.

An extreme example? Maybe. Still, I think such is the sort of person we look like, and are perhaps in danger of becoming, when we get upset over the wrong things, when we focus on the incidental and miss the deeper moral issue. Christian: Don't be that person.

FOX "NEWS" CHRISTIANS

It has long perplexed me. How is this possible? What manner of cognitive dissonance is capable of such amazing mental gymnastics? What devilry, what witchcraft is afoot here? Here there be demons for sure, but where? It was like listening to one's kind and sweet Grandmother talking about kittens and rainbows who suddenly shouts out an expletive. Then it finally dawned on me: this used to be me!

Not only was I a rabid 1980s Moral Majority Republican who actively campaigned for local Republican candidates, I was a 1990s consumer of right-wing talk radio. When Fox "News" debuted in the late 90s, I became a several-hours-per-day viewing addict. Other than occasional movies and sports, it was what I primarily watched in the evenings.

I lived in an echo chamber, a bubble of noisy, white, male, patriotic anger. Who was I angry with? Liberals. Feminists. Democrats. Hillary. Muslims. Obama. Immigrants. Environmentalists. Hillary. College professors. Atheists. Anyone who dared disrespect the flag or America. Hillary. Anyone I didn't think supported law enforcement or the military. Hillary. Anyone I didn't think supported the Second Amendment and gun rights. Oh, and did I say "Hillary"?

While this echo chamber was a combination of fundamentalist/evangelical books/ministries, conservative talk radio, and right-wing websites, the largest of these chambers was Fox News. Fox News had the biggest soap box and the loudest megaphone. And I loved it. At last, some media out there that reinforced and gave voice to what I already believed and thought!

Fox made me feel good about my prejudices. Fox also made me feel aggrieved. Finally, someone who noticed how persecuted I was, what, with people saying, "Happy Holidays" and all. They stood up for God and country ... and white people. Never mind that God, the ground of all being, doesn't need defending or that our country is the most powerful in the world. And how is it that white people, males especially, needed defending? Talk about snowflakes. As if they haven't had the loudest voices and the most power for centuries.

Anyway, Fox also made it clear who the enemies were. I didn't have to think about it too much. It was presented clearly by all the attractive women anchors and the handsome, square-jawed Sean Hannity. These were the good guys; these people were "winners." It was like a show staffed with articulate quarterbacks and cheerleaders. This was the winning news team.

And now, looking back in complete embarrassment, I can say without hesitation it was mostly propagandistic hogwash. I haven't watched Fox News in at least fifteen years. Now, if I ever run across it, if it's on in someone's home, or a bar or restaurant, I watch it like someone might watch monkeys at the zoo, for entertainment. Oh look, they're throwing their feces again.

By the way, yes, I do know there are some decent people at Fox. Just not Roger Ailes, Bill O'Reilly, or any others reprimanded, forced out, or fired over sexual harassment or other egregious actions or remarks.

But my thoughtless intake of Fox News explains so much. It explains how I could be a nice and thoughtful Christian one moment, easily conversant with the Bible and Christian narrative in general, well aware that a primary goal is to defend the poor, the oppressed, the stranger, marginalized, orphan, and widow ... then turn into an angry, right-wing jerk if one brought up the political realm and my supposed "enemies" who, it turns out, were some of those very people we were supposed to defend.

In one moment, I could talk about how the statement "Jesus is Lord" was a political statement. How such a declaration had a deep political meaning, as in, we do not worship emperors, presidents, or nation/states. We are good citizens; we pay our taxes and obey the laws, but we are also citizens of the world and a universal or catholic church. Our true identity is not "American" or "Mexican" (or whatever) but child of God. We are citizens of heaven first, and our brothers and sisters are everywhere. Our ultimate identity is not found in ethnicity, blood, soil, or cultural history.

And, in the next moment, if someone brought up something I thought unpatriotic, I could completely forget all that and respond with ignorant sentiments like, "Hey, this is America, love it or leave it." And don't even get me started about people disrespecting our flag or (gasp!) kneeling during the National Anthem. Yep, my theology would go right out the window as I would bray as loud as the other "America-First-ers" to prove my patriotism. Good job Fox for your expert creation and discipleship of nationalists, i.e., idol worshippers.

It was like Jekyll and Hyde. It was only after I slowly began to wean myself from fundamentalist/evangelical sources of political information, and from the right-wing echo chamber, that I began to see my Mr. Hyde self. And I didn't like what I saw. I stopped watching Fox News and I stopped listening to right-wing talk radio. I went cold turkey.

Afterward, the first thing I noticed was that I was much less angry; or, better, that I was now angry at least at the right things. I began to see the marginalized, the "other," differently. Doing this allowed my views in these areas to align better with the Gospel than Fox. I listened more. I considered the idea that, while I should "seek the welfare of the city," I should also not overlook her faults or shortcomings. And that to do so, even to protest, was not being unpatriotic. In fact, it was the best type of patriotism. Bottom line: Nationalism is heretical and idolatry.

A word of counsel to those still within the fundamentalist/evangelical world or those coming out—to anyone really: Turn off Fox News. It's hardly sound journalism. Get your news from credible, widely respected sources. Especially seek out written sources of news where the bombast, anger, drama, and celebrity so common to television/cable news are removed. Avoid sources from the extreme Right or Left.

We have Protestants (and many variations therein), Catholics, and Orthodox. Unfortunately, we can now add a mutant/heretical variant to all these: Fox News Christians.

Brother, sister: Don't be a Fox News Christian.

TANGLED UP IN RED, WHITE, AND BLUE

The above title is taken from one of the title chapters in Brian Zahnd's book, *Postcards from Babylon*.[2] I encourage everyone to get this book and read it. And then, read it again. If there is a book for our time, it is this one.

As I write, it is Memorial Day weekend in the United States [2019]. This is the day we remember those who died while serving in America's military. We forget that as Christians, our view of war, the military, and killing in the name of the state, are not simple matters. For the serious Christian, there should be no quick lapse into an unthinking or unreflective patriotism during these holidays.

We need to be aware of what we are doing. We must not make an idol of the state. Too many Christians in America practice a false civic religion as if it were integral to, or part of, their Christian faith. It is actually a reflection their faith is misplaced, misdirected, or fundamentally misunderstood. Zahnd writes:

In civic religion, war is always publicly remembered as an act of sacrifice. Public remembrances of war are deeply liturgical because war is memorialized as a sacrament within civic religion. Stanley Hauerwas has taught us that nationalism is a religion with war as its liturgy. The nature of war sacrifice in civic religion is that there must always be more sacrifices. Mars is an insatiable god...Wars waged and especially wars won have always been the most effective way to unite a populace. In times of war the tribe, the nation, the empire rally in unity around the common cause of waging war upon a common enemy.[3]

The problem becomes the nation constantly needs further sacrifices to maintain this unity. Thus, enemies are always present, always around the corner, always on the horizon. And what we are told is that unless we are prepared to wage war, to expend resources, then those who've gone before will have died "in vain." In their memory then, we prepare others, the young mostly, to die also. And so, the sacrament of war is celebrated again and again in the liturgy of the civic religion.

Christians, wherever they find themselves, whether the country of their birth, or transplanted somewhere else, cannot participate in the liturgies of civic religion in any sense of a heart allegiance. We can be respectful of ours or any nation's traditions, pomp, flags, songs, history, and other peculiarities, but always loosely and with reserve. We can practice neighborly love. We can be good, hard-working, honest citizens. We can work for flourishing and healthy communities. If that is what one means by "patriotic," then fine. No problem.

However, if what one means is that "our" nation is special, blessed by God in some sense "others" are not, and worthy in such a way that we would kill even other Christians on its behalf, then such is not patriotism, but nationalism. And nationalism is an idol—a golden calf. And upon its altars we sacrifice our sons and daughters, not to God or each other (ideas we use to comfort ourselves), but to the prince of this world.

Young people are sent by old people to die in wars, the "whys" and "wherefores" they usually don't understand. They often die heroically, not for some high ideal, nation, or misplaced patriotism, but for the brother or sister in arms next to them. Out of a love for each other, they will often give their own lives. Without giving praise to the nations that sent them, to some abstract ideal, resource, or manifest destiny they may have been sent to protect, and that is hardly worthy of their deaths, let us recognize their selfless and noble deaths only in that sense.

More importantly, as peacemakers, as those who claim a gospel of peace, as those who claim to follow the Prince of Peace let us remember, especially on these holidays, that we are part of a Kingdom that includes people from all nations and languages. We are not looking for a city here and now, but for one to come. In the meantime, let us become atheists as far as civil religion and believers in a kingdom of peace.

AMERICA: ISRAEL OR BABYLON?

We recently celebrated the fourth of July; we celebrated our independence. Well, that was the idea anyway. I think most of us celebrated a day off, with fireworks, watermelon, hamburgers, ice cream, soothing adult beverages, and the gathering of families and friends. Whether or not most connected their revelries with our revolution against England and the declaring of our independence, is another matter.

This celebration and other instances of national ritual, habit, or liturgy if you will, brings to mind the founding myths of this republic. One of those myths is the idea that America is a new Israel, a new founding of the people of God, which implies a special relationship and privilege. It carries the idea of a new "chosen" people.

In a *New Republic* essay we read:

Many of the radical Calvinists who resolved to leave England to establish colonies in the newly discovered continent of North America believed themselves to be reenacting the exodus of the Hebrews from bondage in ancient Egypt. Having freely joined in a covenant with God and resolved to build a purified church and holy city in the New World...'[4]

And further on we read:

...the idea that the original colonists had come, with God's aid and assistance, to establish a new Israel on American shores managed to persist...Minister Thomas Thacher of Boston's Old South Church concurred with the judgment, boldly asserting that 'we are the people that do succeed Israel.'

Over the many decades since those first Puritans and Pilgrims, many Christians, and, indeed, even nominally religious people, have embraced this myth, and still do, if even unconsciously and loosely. However, many Christian fundamentalists and some evangelicals, explicitly, believe it to be true. It is from this founding myth, along with the idea that our founding fathers were mostly "evangelical" Christians, that we get the connection made by many Christians that America is a "Christian" nation.[5]

It was probably this founding myth, this idea of being chosen, of being special to God that allowed so many Christians to overlook the two blood red stains that are also a part of our founding and history: the genocide of the original inhabitants (they weren't chosen, I guess) and the practice of slavery that only ended through further bloodshed and civil war.

This isn't to say that America and Americans have not also done and accomplished many good things, but we pass over these two grave national sins at our peril. Every nation is a mixed bag, but a humble nation takes stock of its failures more than its successes. Regardless, it should give one pause, to assume a "national" special relationship to God.

There is, however, another significant nation/city in the Bible—one we should also take notice of before we assume our nation is a type of, or heir to, the "chosen" nation—Israel. That nation/city is Babylon.

If the Church, those who worship the Holy Trinity are a, "chosen race, a royal priesthood, a holy nation, God's own people,"[6] then there is no longer an ethnic race, tied to blood, soil or history, that can be designated as a new Israel or Jerusalem. This "holy nation" is now spread throughout the world and is mixed with and a part of every nation on earth.

Over and against Israel and the Church (the people of God), throughout history there has been a counter-church, a copy, a fake, that is represented by empire—an empire called Babylon.

Here we read: "Babylon is a figure of the city, of the human urge to plant, build, trade, protect oneself against the elements and against outside threats..."[7]

Seems rather harmless, but the inherent tendency is for this counter-community to try and do this as an alternative route, as a way around the selflessness and self-giving inherent in God's economy. As noted by the tower building of Babel, it becomes an attempt to rival God and master the world by violence.

It then becomes a manifestation of the principalities and powers.[8] And we should not assume that Babylon represents a purely secular or anti-religious empire. As to Babylon's characterization in Revelation, here we read:

> ...Therefore Babylon is a symbol of these two enemies [the sociopolitical and religious] in their most deadly form: when the harlot sits on the beast, that is, when the false religious entities, and in particular apostate Christianity, attempt to use or work with the existing political and social powers to destroy the church of Christ...[9]

Of particular interest, in light of the Religious Right and their alliance with the Republican Party, is the reason for Babylon's destruction and judgment. From the same source we read:

...[the reason] is because 'from the wine of the rage of her immorality all the nations have drunk, and the kings of the earth committed sexual immorality with her, and the merchants of the earth became wealthy by the power of her luxurious sensuality...'[10]

We might interpret this to mean, the religious aspect of Babylon was in bed with the kings, with the political powers. They were sleeping together. While the merchants were made rich, these two shared the same bed and we hear nothing of their concern for the weak, the poor, or the outcast. After all, part of the merchant's commerce included, "slaves—and human lives."[11]

I think every great nation, power, or city/state, now and in all of history has been tempted to be Babylon. Perhaps there is no clear answer to whether or not America is more like an Israel or a Babylon, other than, it is always a possibility to act as either. I leave that to the reader. In my personal opinion, as America is currently situated, to me, we look more like Babylon than Israel.

SOME OF MY BEST FRIENDS ARE THE LEAST OF THESE

Christian fundamentalists and evangelicals face a big dilemma whenever they read Matthew 25: 31-46. In their minds, a single decision, at a specific moment in time, will determine a person's eternal destiny. In their view, anything else a person does in life is really secondary to whether or not they made a personal decision for Jesus. Ultimately, they believe this is what a person will be judged upon. The problem is that none of that lines up with Matthew 25: 31-46.

To further complicate things, many fundamentalists and evangelicals will tell us that focusing too much on people's physical needs is dangerous and can distract us from focusing upon their true need: The salvation of their souls. In their theology, the Good News, the Gospel, is only about the salvation of souls and a person's eternal destination—anything is secondary. To focus on people's physical needs is, in their view a "social gospel" and is, at best, a distraction—at worst, it's even dangerous.

We will say again, however, that the Good News *is social justice* and is such before it is ever anything about a life in the sweet ever-after. The Gospel is first what is noted in Luke's gospel,[12] before it is ever anything about going to heaven—which, as N.T. Wright has noted, is mostly misunderstood to begin with anyway.[13]

I would like us to consider the area of social justice (bad words to conservative fundamentalist/evangelicals—for many, it gets them more upset than the word Trump used to describe what he liked to grab when, "courting" women), in the light of Matthew 25:31-46, the well-known "least of these" passage—because it is so pertinent to the discussion. There is a common refrain from conservative evangelicals when it comes to this passage. They are quick to point out that the "least of these" means either Christians or missionary Christians. Then, they are quick to do something else.

Knowing full well this appears to be a rather self-centered reading and one indifferent to non-Christians, they let us know that, yes, everywhere else in the Bible we are told to care for the poor and marginalized, regardless. Still, they just don't want us to read *this passage* that way. This always strikes me as the type of qualification we might hear from the self-unaware white guy, who, when caught in a prejudicial remark or objection, assures us that some of their best friends are, non-white. "But still...," they add.

To me, the objection seems disingenuous and self-unaware—especially in light of current events and disagreements over how we should understand social justice. This may be the real objection: I don't like the fact this passage seems to bolster the progressive case for the priority of social justice—a priority, mind you—even linked to our salvation. No, the person objecting always wants us to know, they just really, really care about correct and proper interpretation. Oh, okay. Got it.

Let's consider such, then. There are several reasons to believe the passage is speaking of people in general, and not just Christians. These reasons are echoed in other sources, but I've taken these primarily from New Testament scholar Arland J. Hultgren, and his book *The Parables of Jesus*.[14]

Reason 1: The interpretation that the least of these are Christians/missionaries is, textually, based upon making a connection between the terms "least of these," "brothers and sisters" and similar terms elsewhere in Matthew and the New Testament. However, as noted by Hultgren: "While cross-referencing is essential in the study of terms, it should be subservient to the study of the overall structure and content of the text at hand."[15]

And then Hultgren quotes E. Watson: "No one, reading Matt 25:31-46 in isolation, would suppose that its subject is the treatment of Christian evangelists."[16] And, I would add, Christians in general. Side note: Please then, don't make so much fuss over a "plain reading of the text" in other cases, if you are not willing to make it here.

Reason 2: The term "least" of these (ἐλάχιστoς) can be used of a disciple or Christ follower, but it is better suited to denote anyone who, in the estimation of people in general, are considered small in rank and importance. This would include those in need physically who for whatever reason find themselves on the outside, the unfortunate ones. Hultgren writes:

> ...it is precisely because they are not his disciples in any obvious way that Jesus can call them 'the least' of his 'brothers.' They are 'the least' purely because of God's special favor for them, which Jesus here declares. It is certainly much simpler—

looking for the plainest meaning of the text—to consider 'the least' as referring to persons who are actually and continuously despised and neglected in the course of common life, and then declared Jesus' brothers by grace alone, than to think of them as disciples of Jesus, who may or may not be despised at any time or place.[17]

The point of the first two reasons is that the interpretation conservatives are trying to make based on how the terms are used elsewhere, the textual case, is not as strong a case as they seem to think. And, this is the *primary reason* for their interpretation.

Reason 3: A common defense of the interpretation that the "least of these" refers only to Christians is that this interpretation is the most common in antiquity. Hultgren responds:

It has been said that the interpretation favored here... [that the least of these are people in general] ...is actually not very old, and that it became important only in the nineteenth century. That in itself would not be cause for rejecting it. But it should be pointed out that it has been expressed from early times, for example, in the writings of Cyprian, Commodianus, and John Chrysostom, in the Rule of St. Benedict, and occasionally in the works of Jerome.[18]

Reason 4: In relation to reason 3, Hultgren also points out that the interpretation the least of these refers to all people and not just Christians, "prevails in various studies of NT ethics."[19]

Reason 5: Finally, here is, I think, the strongest reason for the interpretation that the least are people in general and not just Christians. I will quote Hultgren at length:

The persons on the right and left are astonished to hear that they have, or have not, served the king who speaks to them. If the persons on the right had served the representatives of the king—feeding them, clothing them, welcoming them (regardless of their being strangers), and visiting them while sick or in prison—and if the representatives had been missionary disciples of Jesus, why would those on the right find that out only at the last judgment? If we are to adopt the view that "the least" are disciples, it follows that the last judgment passage portrays a scene in which the Son of man rewards those who knowingly served him in the world, that is, those who had received and served disciples who came in his name. But that is *precisely what we do not have.* (emphasis added)

He goes on in the same section:

They did not know that the persons they neglected to serve came to them in the name of Jesus. And if the unfortunates never identified themselves, how are they to be distinguished from any other unfortunates of the world?[20]

Any textual or exegetical case, the use of terms, would have to give way to what is clearly the best and most cogent hermeneutical understanding of the text given the "overall structure and content of the text..." I would suggest then, that content, interior consistency, structure, and context, should over-ride conclusions derived mostly from the comparison of terms and their usage elsewhere. Further, conclusions, which go against the entire scope of Scripture when it comes to the identification of the poor and marginalized should be thrown out.

There are many other reasons to believe the "least of these" refers to people in general, in all times and places, and not just or only Christians. However, the above five reasons are some of the more compelling. I readily admit the passage could be read the way conservative fundamentalist/evangelicals believe it should be read, and such is a reasonable interpretation. I just don't think it is the best one or, indeed, the correct one for all the reasons noted and others.

Conservative fundamentalists/evangelicals protest, it seems to me, a little too much when it comes to this text. On one hand, they are quick to qualify their objection by telling us they know the preponderance of Scripture compels us to do what is spoken of in Matthew 25: 31-46, for all people, not only Christians or the "Godly." But, on the other hand, even admitting such, they assert Matthew 25:31-46 is the exception.

To that, we should point out not only the inconsistency and not very subtle attempt to slight the social justice movement, but also that their interpretation is not very compelling in most respects, including textually. But, more importantly, it is not very compelling hermeneutically, nor if we compare it to the entire ethical sweep and arc of Scripture as a whole.

THE UNBEARABLE LIGHTNESS OF EVANGELICAL TRIGGERS

I've written before of how fundamentalist/evangelicals get upset over the wrong things. And new examples seem to come unbidden all the time. I suppose this is what happens when fundamentalist/evangelical pastors and leaders outsource their discipleship and teaching duties to Fox News, Breitbart, and other right-wing propaganda outlets.

The average fundamentalist/evangelical pastor has no idea what he's up against. They get a couple hours on Sunday and maybe an hour or two during the week to teach and disciple their people, but these "news" outlets get to do the same thing several hours a day, seven days a week, year-round. There's no competition. These poor pastors, leaders, and teachers think they are discipling and shaping their flocks, but their congregants show up with that goal already accomplished. They then "hear" everything the pastor is saying through the framework already provided them by the likes of Sean Hannity and Tucker Carlson.

Sadly, we know there are many pastors/priests, leaders, teachers, and professors, who have themselves been discipled by these right-wing channels of propaganda. At some point, they reinterpreted much of what they had learned so it would comport with the new understanding given them by people who, upon cursory inspection, are nothing more than political ideologues taking advantage of peoples' prejudices and fears. Sadly, it's worked.

For decades, Christian ethics and morality in evangelical circles have been reinterpreted to fit a modern right-wing ideology, rather than the rich and deep tradition going back 2000 years and longer. And now the chickens are coming home to roost. When we outsource our teaching of ethics to hucksters and pseudo-intellectuals, we get these sorts of responses and triggers. When we have been fed a steady diet of the ethical equivalent of hot dogs and Twinkies in their moral nutritional value, we shouldn't be surprised at the outcome.

For an example of what I mean, take the time former President Trump came under criticism from fundamentalists and evangelicals for using some salty language during some campaign event.[21] These Christians were very upset and triggered by his language.

Let me get this straight: We're not triggered by the abject dishonesty and lack of integrity, paying off porn stars, the serial adultery, the tacit support of those trying to disrupt our democracy, the obstruction of justice, the sexism, the racism, putting children in cages and separating families, the bullying, the name-calling, and the crass narcissism of an insecure, small, angry, and petty man.

No, none of that. We're not upset this man, who is a cross between Archie Bunker and Michael Scott, is a national and international embarrassment. We're not upset he's a propagator of insane conspiracy theories and goes out of his way to divide people and push them farther apart. Nope. We're not upset he defends dictators and murderers while calling into question leaders of democracies, his own intelligence agencies, the FBI, and our allies around the world. Nope, we're fine with all that.

What will trigger us however, what will really upset us, what will make us call our congressperson or senator, is, yep, you got it: cussing. And God forbid anyone throw in the Lord's name—then we will really get our boxers in a wad. We will rush by the people truly offended and hurt by Trump's racism, sexism, and other weightier ethical failures, to wag our fingers in his face. Like he cares. Folks, if this other stuff doesn't bother him, do you really think he cares one whit that his normal way of speaking and thinking offends you somehow? Please. You've been had. He knows what you are—and as to what it may cost him, it's just a quibble over price at this point.

We have a segment of evangelicals out there with an understanding of ethics and morality on par with a child's understanding of physics. Their sense of scale, of what matters, of moral weight in the balance of things, is seriously off. It is unbearably light, flimsy, and air like. Since it cannot bear any weight, we get the ridiculous responses from people triggered more by Trump's cussing than his racism/sexism or his being just a generally terrible person. This is where we are in America right now and it's really a damn shame.

IS SEPARATING THE GOSPEL FROM SOCIAL JUSTICE A SIGN OF WHITE PRIVILEGE?

I'm suspicious. When I read or hear something put out by those most critical of the social justice movement, I often wonder if the true reasons for their opposition are more cultural than theological.

There are obvious reasons I'm suspicious. The overwhelming

number of voices critical of social justice are white, male, and evangelical/fundamentalist. This statement[22] is a good example. The great majority have rarely, if ever, had to deal with the same cultural, social, political and economic issues as their non-white or female counter parts.

In their minds, I think most of these voices genuinely believe they are defending the "gospel." However, I'm just not sure what "gospel" they mean. Yes, I know they think it is the "historic" gospel, but the churches with much longer traditions (Eastern Orthodox for example), would certainly not agree with their view of "historic," let alone their view of the gospel.

Besides, a gospel that is only about avoiding a future hell isn't good news for those already living in one. The question remains: Why the need to pull them apart, to dichotomize gospel and social justice? Those defending the priority of the gospel, of course, talk about the need for works of mercy, charity, and justice. However, they want to make sure we don't identify those works as the gospel, but as the result of the gospel.

Is this for fear of a works-based salvation? It shouldn't be. Those who think social justice is intrinsic to the gospel also believe we are saved by grace, or at the least don't try and separate grace and works. In other words, they believe both James (2:17) and Paul. They also see the gospel, salvation, and social justice in the light of Matthew 25:31-46.

Is it for fear we will no longer evangelize, but simply be decent people who side with the "least of these" and work for justice? Interesting. What if being decent people who cared (in action, not just sentiment) about the least of these, turned out to be true evangelism? Regardless, this is hardly a valid fear.

Is it based on the idea we must change hearts before we can change culture and law? They certainly don't believe that when it comes to abortion or the LGBT community. They don't seem to believe it when it comes to illegal immigration or religious liberty issues. In these areas, it's all about legislating and law—hearts be damned.

They do seem to believe this (hearts before laws) when it comes to social justice, racism, and sexism though. Here, rather than the law, they believe hearts need to change first. While non-white communities and women suffer, lament, and protest, they would rather talk about hearts than laws. Interesting. Why is that?

Is it the fear that "social justice" is some sort of code for leftist or progressive politics? Is it the long-held fear of Marxism and Communism? If so, I suppose a response predicated upon battles played out in the 1940s and 1950s is what happens when so many people are that out of touch with the present moment. The past is all they have.

There is a reason non-white communities were much more open to leftist political and economic thought, especially prior to the 1970s. Many did not feel included or able to participate within a white world of political and economic domination. It's hard to feel "free" when one begins to learn the entire Jim Crow system is weighted against them.

In my opinion, the true issue is white privilege. I would answer my query (my title) in the affirmative. I think the reason these voices want to separate the gospel and social justice is because the great majority of them have rarely experienced an absence of social justice in their personal lives, and therefore it's just not an issue they care about.

In their minds, adding social justice to the gospel complicates the current formula and brings a haunting and no doubt unwanted sting to the conscience. Rather than a simple prayer and cognitive theological affirmation, it requires seeing the world from the perspective of the "least of these." It requires living and working toward a world where "the least" become fewer and fewer.

As long as we can keep the gospel and salvation in the

abstract, in some metaphysical/spiritual location, where they initially don't touch this life, then we never really have to change. We never have to work toward making the good news concrete for those who suffer in this life while we too often, rest comfortably waiting for heaven.

But to keep the gospel and social justice together means acknowledging white privilege. It means understanding how we were (are) part of the machinery creating the "least of these," to begin with, the very ones upon which our salvation now depends (Oh, the irony). They are, after all, Jesus. Whatever we did for them (or didn't do), we did for Jesus.[23]

For far too many in this life, a gospel separated from social justice is not good news. If it's not good news for all of us, then it's not genuinely good news for any of us. It's a truncated gospel—a gospel too small.

Here is how Jesus described the gospel—the good news:

> And he came to Nazareth, where he had been brought up. And as was his custom, he went to the synagogue on the Sabbath day, and he stood up to read. And the scroll of the prophet Isaiah was given to him. He unrolled the scroll and found the place where it was written, "The Spirit of the Lord is upon me, because he has anointed me to proclaim good news to the poor. He has sent me to proclaim liberty to the captives and recovering of sight to the blind, to set at liberty those who are oppressed, to proclaim the year of the Lord's favor." And he rolled up the scroll and gave it back to the attendant and sat down. And the eyes of all in the synagogue were fixed on him. And he began to say to them, "Today this Scripture has been fulfilled in your hearing."[24]

If one takes the entire Biblical narrative as a whole and not just proof texts from St. Paul's writings, there is no separation of the gospel and social justice. And if one is longing for justice, such is easy to see. If one is not, then the gospel is first, an abstract concept about salvation; secondly, it's a ticket to a future heaven, and only thirdly about our actual life here and now. But only a person with little worries in this life can afford to view it that way, to see the gospel and social justice as separate.

The rest don't have that privilege.

BIBLICAL JUSTICE IS SOCIAL JUSTICE

Running through the theological framework of fundamentalism and evangelicalism, perhaps even the Protestant tradition, is the discernible need to dichotomize everything. Of course, it's a feature of modernity. Whether it's works vs. grace, scripture vs. tradition, predestination vs. free will, etc., it has to be either one or the other, hardly ever *both/and*. We see two concepts often being needlessly opposed or separated. Something we see presently are those who wish to oppose biblical justice to social justice.

I would counter that biblical justice *is* social justice. Justice is both vertical (God and humanity) and horizontal (community-person-to- person). In the horizontal sense, it of course always touches the political because it is bound up in law and culture. Still, social justice is not a modern left- or right-wing formulation, but a biblical teaching and one inherent in the scriptural narrative and Christian tradition. With that view in mind, I would like to address a blog post published on the religious platform *Patheos* in 2019.[25]

The writer asserts:

> However, life and Scriptures have taught me that social justice is different than biblical justice. Christ did not come just for "the triply oppressed" or the "most marginalized people". He came for the sinner, which means Caesar, you, and me.

Why are these (the oppressed and marginalized) and those who don't fall into those categories opposed to each other, or separated? Yes, of course, Christ came for all—for sinners. So what? That is completely beside the point. No progressive Christian I am aware of believes Jesus only came for the oppressed. This separation is especially egregious in light of the way Jesus describes the gospel (as noted in the previous chapter) and why he was sent:

> The Spirit of the Lord is upon me, because he has anointed me to proclaim good news to the poor. He has sent me to proclaim liberty to the captives and recovering of sight to the blind, to set at liberty those who are oppressed, to proclaim the year of the Lord's favor" (Luke 4:16-21).

The writer goes on to assert there is no identity politics in the Bible. Again, so what? Who said there was? This is a red herring. So too is the assertion that, "Jesus did not die for only certain groups in human society." Again, who said that he did? No one—no credible person anyway. The writer is using the concept of biblical justice to argue against her own false conception of a leftist politics, not social justice.

Moving on, we read:

> Our biggest priority as Christ followers is not to achieve "social justice" or "equality" on Earth as my brethren on the left would have us believe. That is a low bar for Christians to set for our goal.

According to the passage I just cited, Jesus didn't think it was a low bar. If a person has been denied social justice or equality, it's certainly not a low bar to them either. Every Christian should be seeking (whether it is achieved on earth or not, which is, by the way, irrelevant) social justice and equality for those who don't have it yet. Think about the 1960s' Civil Rights Era. Imagine at that time telling black communities in places like Mississippi that to help them was a "low bar" and we had other far more important goals to attain. It would be just as disgraceful and disobedient to do the same now.

She then writes: "Fighting for the oppressed and giving voice to the voiceless is a wonderful thing to do if we are led by the Holy Spirit."

We are led by the Spirit to do such. It's not only "wonderful" to do, it is absolutely required. From Genesis to Revelation, it is required. It's not an option. It would literally take another entire post to list all the scripture passages that tell us we are required to advocate for the oppressed and be a voice for the voiceless (or, how about just reading the entire Old Testament). I can't think of a single respected or credible Christian teacher or theologian who would argue otherwise.

Further:

> Westerners (whether white or people of color, Christians or non-Christians) who aim for this kind of "justice" in society are actually spreading more division and destruction because it is done in a spirit of anger and self-righteousness.

No, it is actual racism and sexism that spreads division and destruction. Does that even need to be said? The claim that those who point it out, even if done incorrectly, are the ones causing division is pretty rich. I'm sure many thought Martin Luther King Jr. was self-righteous and angry sometimes too. Was he then spreading division and destruction?

Are there those working for social/biblical justice who are sometimes angry and self-righteous? Sure. Again, so what? While there is no need for self-righteousness, sometimes there is a need for anger. Read some of the Old (First) Testament prophets. Jesus seemed fairly angry when he cleansed the

Temple, an event with a decidedly social justice component since the poor were being taken advantage of.

I would rather have a person fighting for the oppressed and being a voice for the voiceless but doing it poorly, than a person who doesn't do it at all or downplays it like this writer. Besides, there are angry and self-righteous people on both sides. It has nothing to do with whether or not their arguments are true or their goal just. It's simply another red herring.

Look, if the writer were objecting to a perceived anger and self-righteousness on the part of social justice advocates, and not social justice itself, then the entire post should have been about tone, emotion, and communication issues rather than downplaying social justice by contrasting it with biblical justice. It seems clear that social justice is precisely the writer's true objection, and not these other issues.

The writer then mistakes her history with communism for the current conversation regarding social justice, as if they were the same thing. They are not the same. No credible progressive Christian I am aware of is advocating for a type of "social justice" that resembles the authoritarian/totalitarian versions of either the left or right from decades past.

They are speaking about racism and sexism. They are speaking about economic justice—the indecent gap between the rich and poor. They are talking about health care, poverty, the criminal justice system and education. Their methods are directed toward both hearts and the law but done peacefully and through democratic means. Those are good goals, just goals, even if pursued sometimes poorly. If one doesn't like the way it is being done, then do it better.

Social justice is biblical justice. When we strive for social justice, when we act for the "least of these," when we love our neighbor (which includes social justice) we are giving them Jesus. We are following scripture. If all one sees is "anger" on the part of those who are trying to help the oppressed and marginalized, one is missing both Jesus and the "least of these."

Separating biblical justice from social justice may salve our conscience, but it certainly doesn't help anyone else.

DEAD MAN WALKING

Indulge me. When a rock is dropped in a pond, waves are set in motion. We see or feel them in time, based on distance. I want to suggest there have been two events in recent times, which are portentous for what we call evangelicalism. These two events— among others—are like rocks dropped in a pond. Their waves are coming; they're just not here yet.

These two events, I believe, amount to a death sentence of sorts—one handed down, but not yet executed. My sense is that the coming waves, which depict the ideas and consequences set in motion by those events, portend the death of modern, American evangelicalism.

Yes, I know the supposed death of evangelicalism or fundamentalism has been foretold many times over the years. We should smile if those of that tradition were to echo Twain, that the reports of their deaths have been greatly exaggerated. And I should be clear, rarely does any significant historical movement entirely die out. Obviously, I'm speaking metaphorically. By "death," I simply mean cultural irrelevance and loss of influence. Additionally, I readily admit I could be wrong.

I also know that movements and traditions are capable of change. It's possible that enough leaders and thinkers in that tradition will also see what's coming, what's on the horizon, and move people to change—to see and think differently—to act differently. So, there are many wild cards in play here. I give no great weight to any prophetic gifting I may presume here, other than to say—it's also possible I may be onto something.

With those caveats, I will stride forth. Modern American

evangelicalism (and its cousin, fundamentalism) could be considered, in my opinion, dead men walking–but here I speak mostly of evangelicalism. Alive, yes, but the clock is ticking. Some evangelicals may read this and respond, "But the gates of hell will never prevail over the church, and the gospel will never pass away or be defeated!" Rah, rah.

Yes, I agree. But that's not what I'm suggesting. The truth is that traditions, denominations, movements, schools of thought, and theologies, do in fact die or fade into history. The vagaries of history and events in general can coincide in such a way as to lead them ultimately to their demise. If anyone doubts this, simply read some history books chronicling either Christian history or religion in general.

Again, I'm not speaking of the Church Universal, but of historical traditions, splinters, and streams arising in temporal time. Only pride would ever lead a religious group or tradition produced by an enormously complex matrix of historical events, to believe they were somehow a permanent feature of temporal time—blessed above all others—as if similar events could not arise in the future.

Of the two events I speak of, one is well-known and one more hidden, one political and the other theological. The public, political, and better-known event or stone dropped in the water, was the "election" of Trump.

Of this first event, not much needs to be written that hasn't already. This was such a grievous, unwise, small, petty, ignorant, and immature act of hypocrisy on the part of evangelicals, it still staggers the imagination and even the slightest rational mind. After all, what tradition or movement could possibly teach for decades the importance of personal morality, integrity, honesty, and character in political leaders and then turn on a dime and vote for the exact opposite—all to say yes to the devil's tempta-tion of political power? This was the first shout of, "dead man walking."

The second, more theological and less public event, was the publication of two books. One book[26] was popular (infamously!) and written for a general audience, while the other[27] is probably less known to the general public and written more for the serious reader or academic audience. However, both make the same claim. To wit: Love wins, and all shall be saved. Both books, in their own way, come to the same conclusion. As to the end of all things, the cosmos, everything, and every person—all will be redeemed, even as if by fire. This was the second call of "dead man walking."

The first event revealed the ethical, social, political, and intellectual poverty of evangelicalism. The many warnings given over the years, in general, were either not heeded or misunderstood. The continued Babylonian captivity to consumerism, nationalism, blind obedience to one political party, the "practical," worship as entertainment, and numbers over spiritual formation/ deep theological reflection has led to a number of problems. Foremost, a people willing to vote for—or tacitly agree with by remaining silent—an ethically challenged, ignorant clown.

The second event undercuts the very raison d'être of the evangelical tradition. What does the verbal proclamation of the gospel, witnessing, sharing—the telling of others about Jesus and salvation mean now, once we remove the specter of hell as an infinite consequence for failing to "accept" Christ in this temporal, finite earthly life? When the edifice is built upon the idea the neighborhood is on fire, but the inhabitants are unaware—when one's job, one's whole existence, is to warn them the house is on fire so they might be "saved"; and when we then find that the edifice is cracked, well…what then?

Having said that, the proclamation of the gospel, evangelism, and making disciples will go on (I hasten to reassure you, lest evangelicals' shudder at my words). We are clearly tasked with such. However, once these books have been digested (along with many others), we will see these tasks in a completely different light—or at least we should. Evangelism will become what it has always been—a lived announcement of the news already announced here:

> The Spirit of the Lord is upon me, because he has anointed me to bring good news to the poor. He has sent me to proclaim release to the captives and recovery of sight to the blind, to let the oppressed go free, to proclaim the year of the Lord's favor.[28]

The good news isn't "turn or burn." That's the message of a sociopath. The good news, as just noted by Christ in Luke's gospel, is truly good as it announces a new paradigm, a new Kingdom, a way of life that subverts whatever structures and powers were in place—including our own hearts—that first led to the creation of the categories of persons he identifies, the poor, the captive, the blind and the oppressed.

Evangelism is primarily something lived and not just verbally "shared." One cannot bring such a message without doing something about these very categories making up the audience, the recipients of this good news. Otherwise, we are hypocrites. This is something evangelicals have always reversed, putting mouth before foot, with a view toward a supposed future hell, rather than any present ones.

The good news isn't about saving people from a future hell of eternal torture, but about the announcement hell has been harrowed and all the gates and locks have been destroyed by the death and resurrection of Christ. The "how" or strategy of this announcement is in the loving and serving of others, especially our enemies—thus, the Kingdom comes. What will evangelicals do when they realize the so-called "social gospel," is really... just...the gospel?

Now, again, I may be wrong about all this. I probably sound like that bothered, troubled mind, Nietzsche, and his madman:

> "I have come too early," he said then; "my time has not come yet. The tremendous event is still on its way, still travelling—it has not yet reached the ears of men. Lightning and thunder require time, the light of the stars requires time, deeds require time even after they are done, before they can be seen and heard. This deed is still more distant from them than the distant stars—and yet they have done it themselves."[29]

Still, I have the eerie sense that just like the character played by Bruce Willis in the movie *Sixth Sense,* the white (yes, I add white here at the end for accuracy) evangelical tradition, as presently situated, is dead. They just don't know it yet.

INTRODUCTION TO CHAPTER FIVE

As far as I know, no one has ever been reasoned into, or logic(ed) into...love. We use the word "falling" or "fell." Think of that. We were walking along, and we encountered something so breathtaking, so moving, so noticeable, we fell down. We forgot where we were for a moment. We left our bodies and were floating. It was almost as if someone had placed one of those cartoon black circles in front of us, which became a hole we fell into.

None of us, I doubt, were shown an algebraic formula that equaled...love. Our significant other didn't come over one day and say: "I've done the literal math. We belong together." There was no empirical investigation or scientific experiment done in a laboratory with control measures in place.

No, love is a mystery. We don't understand it. We can't replicate it or explain it in any sort of scientific or mathematical fashion. And yet, it is more important to us than anything. We live and die for what we love. It's the reason we get up in the morning and go to bed at night. It's the reason we live, work, and play. But few of us know what it is or can explain it very well.

The Christian narrative tells us that God is love. Not that God loves…or is loving. No, God "*is*" love. Ontologically, at the core of existence, of being, is…love. God. The core of existence isn't a random violence, hate, or indifference. It's not a competitive survival of the fittest. No, those are shadows. Those are the echoes of a broken world. The reality, the core, when one has gone behind every curtain, every false front, and finally gets to the end of all things, there is…love. Or, God.

That, however, is experienced and learned. It's not anything one can prove mathematically or in a scientific, empirical, experiment. It is learned through beauty. It is learned and experienced through the true, the good, and the beautiful. Whenever those qualities/aspects/realities are reflected in action, language, literature, poetry, music, drama, or art (even science), we learn and experience the truth of existence.

However, we are always learning and experiencing such through a broken world. Thus, in the music world, the blues, may invoke great love and beauty, but it does so from a perspective that has suffered and experienced pain. Art, of any sort, often makes us cry. Why? We may cry because we are overwhelmed by beauty—it may be a good cry. But it also may be tears of grief or sadness. We cry because we've been shown the truth of a broken and scarred existence.

One of my favorite writers, Dostoyevsky, asserted that: *Beauty will save the world*. I think this to be true. Pure, modern, Western, rational argument, PowerPoint presentations, diagrams, equations, experiments, pure logic, and all the forms of communication employed and given priority in our time…will not save the world. A paradox: Beauty may employ all those. However, at the end of the day, it was beauty that prevailed. Not the method or vehicle used.

Once we leave the fundamentalist/evangelical world, we

often wonder: How do we share our faith now? What does evangelism look like now?

My humble suggestion is that we do evangelism through the beauty of our lives, our actions most importantly. In our lives, actions, words, and in what we produce culturally, if those are good, beautiful, and true, the world will be transformed. It will not be transformed by our abstract opinions, theologies, correct rational arguments, mathematical equations, or a supposed pure logic.

I claim no expertise as to beauty. All I can do is speak out of my experience and life. This chapter has to do with speaking from the area of the poetic, the true, good, and beautiful, which is the real. If the reader has encountered love in their life, they know what that was like and what it did for them. Go and do likewise.

CHAPTER FIVE

OPEN RANGE—THE POETIC

THE POETIC AND THE REAL

Modernity[1] tells a story about what is "real." And that story goes something like this:

Before the Enlightenment, before modern science, people were superstitious and believed fables, myths, and fairytales, which included religion as well. In fact, they were all of one piece. Were they interesting and imaginative? Sure. Were they colorful and even beautiful, some of them? Certainly. Were there some historical, cultural, and sociological strands of information contained within, that were at least helpful in giving a "true" or "factual" picture of their time? Probably. But, most importantly, they were false and not true in any empirical, scientific, or factual sense. And for the modern, that is the only description of "true" or "real" one is allowed or will be tolerated.

This is what is meant when we hear of the "disenchantment"[2] of the world. Modernity broke the spell if you will. In a world understood as pure nature where there is only the physical and material, such became devoid of spirit and no longer participated in the spiritual or divine. The material world was bifurcated. Maybe there was a spiritual/heavenly plane of existence, but it was "up there" or somewhere other than "here."

Disenchantment meant that a tree was *just* a tree now. A rock was *just* a rock. People, the ocean, the night sky, the snow-covered forest, the sunrise, the sunset—all the aspects of the material/physical world were reduced to pure matter-in-motion, over time and nothing more (If we were to speak "truthfully" and "factually"). This doesn't mean that modern people, especially the atheist/agnostic, lost their sense of the aesthetic/poetic, or had no sense of the beautiful and good, it only means they saw such as metaphorically descriptive, but not true in essence or ontologically.

Modernity, after the Enlightenment, swept the fairies, elves, ghosts, witches, little people, spirits, and gods out the door and then closed it tight. It was okay if people believed all these were "out there" somewhere now, but they were no longer in the house—so to speak. We could still talk about these mythical spirits, creatures, and gods, but only as products of the imagination or former tenants. The spirits no longer inhabited the forests, rivers, and mountains, nor infused the physical world with their presence or powers.

To speak of any of these facets of existence, in any way that went beyond their mere physical appearance and substance, was to speak poetically. To say the wind is whispering, or the sky crying, is to speak metaphorically, poetically. And such is fine. But what modernity will not tolerate is to say at the same time, that one is speaking truthfully. For modernity, the poetic can never be true, at least, in any important or significant sense.

To break the spell of modernity, we must again speak poetically and at the same time, let it be known we are also speaking *truthfully*. We are saying something more real, something more substantive, than simply noting pieces of reductionist information—that matter is in motion and existence is purely material/physical.

As we have already been discussing, this is what the fundamentalist/evangelical world doesn't understand either. They think any reading of Scripture that isn't literal (meaning empirical, scientific, historical fact), is false or misguided—which is another reason they are more modern than they realize. When someone hears that the first chapters of Genesis may be speaking of something other than a literal, scientific description of God's creating, what they hear is that it might as well be false then, since a poetic reading (or any reading that is not literal), cannot be true. An atheist or secular/modern person could not have said it better and is in complete agreement with them. Such an irony seems always lost on the fundamentalist/evangelical.

Cher was in a charming and funny movie in the 1980's entitled *Moonstruck*.[3] I love that movie. I suppose we could describe the movie as one that depicts people, is set in New York, and that at one point, a full moon is shown/discussed...for some reason. That might be how modernity would review the movie.

But we must (and most do) see the movie differently. We must speak of being "moonstruck"—and what that means. To speak this way is to speak the truth of the moon and its perception, in a much more real way than we ever could by listing facts about the moon, i.e., how big the moon is, how far from the earth, orbit, topography, type of soil, or any other mere measurement we could note. Are all those "facts" true? Of course. Are they important? Of course. But there is something truer, more real, than those mere facts.

There is the enchantment of being "moonstruck" and all the mystery, depth, and the sublime contained (but not held) therein by that word. It is the difference between speaking descriptively (mere facts) and truthfully (poetically).

We must re-enchant the world, which is simply to say we

must point out that which already is—it is right in front of us.
The world, existence, is enchanted. There is a depth to things.
There is a mystery to things that science or empirical "fact"
cannot capture. And when we speak of that depth and mystery,
we speak the truth, the real.

As Elizabeth Barrett Browning put it:

> "...Earth's crammed with heaven,
> And every common bush afire with God;
> But only he who sees, takes off his shoes,
> The rest sit round it and pluck blackberries,
> And daub their natural faces unaware..."

THE FIRST POET

I came across this quote from C. Day Lewis (the father of the
famous actor) who is describing what poetry is and does:

> A way of using words to say things which could not possibly be
> said in any other way, things which in a sense do not exist till
> they are born...in poetry.[4]

I think this very apt and true. And true no matter what form
that poetry takes, whether song, portions of script, or prose. The
poetic is able to capture feelings, moods, moments, even time
itself, and communicate those aspects in ways that bring them
to life in the reader or hearer. We are transported in those
moments.

I was especially struck by the creative aspect—not in the
artistic sense, but in the sense of bringing forth something that
did not exist. Unless you are an alchemist or magician, you can
change, fashion, and transform material, but not call it into existence. As to the material, we only discover, change, or fashion
what was already present in atoms and molecules/energy.

An idea however, a fictional place, scene, or character, is brought into existence. The idea or character may be based upon or revealed in a material reality, or derive from other ideas or characters, but it still retains a sort of independent existence that was not prior, like the material or physical. There are many stories with characters based on young boys, but there is only one Tom Sawyer.

There are many types of country western songs, where there are many similarities, like the chords used, meter, key, voicing, instruments used, and so on. However, there is something about "He Stopped Loving Her Today,"[5] or "Crazy"[6] that just do not exist in other songs. And this aspect goes beyond just the level of talent, skill, or ability inherent in the song, song writer, musicians, or singer.

The same is true of any musical genre. A song is like other songs, but it is not those other songs. There is something about the poetic that is unique to each creation, in the sense that, while it is similar to other poetic pieces, it has its own existence and integrity. The author, the creator, brought it forth. Before, it did not exist. Now, it does.

We might think, but it is fiction—it isn't "real." I would suggest it is even more "real" (see previous chapters) than an atom or molecule. How? Because anything created that touches on truth, goodness, or beauty is eternal. It reflects something that existed before the material and informs, suspends, and explains the material. Thus, it is more "real" if you will. Staring at a Periodic Table of Elements (devoid of any context) is unlikely to move us deeply, but a poem, story, or song about the elements often may. In my view, this makes the poetic the more substantive reality.

Isn't this what God did? Isn't creation, existence, —a poem? Except God is able to bring even the material into existence out of nothing, but still make it poetic as we "read" it, experience it, in the sunrise, sunset, waterfall, or rainbow. What is the night sky, with its hanging diamonds, sparks of light, and milky haze, but a poem. Being made in the image of God, we do the same with the poetic or any of the areas we put under the umbrella of the creative arts and perhaps this applies even to science or any endeavor.

God was the first poet and we are all poets in our own ways. We can't help it—it is what we are and do. Anything we do that touches on truth, goodness, and beauty is a poem (no matter what form it takes) that calls into existence aspects of those three that did not exist before. And these will continue to exist, even though the heavens fall.

THE GLORY IN FRONT OF US

One mark of modernity is dichotomy. The world was split asunder when the material and the spiritual were thought, one to be here, and the other, out there...somewhere. From theological and philosophical moves made in the fourteenth century, a two-story universe was constructed.[7] Thereafter, faith and reason, science, and religion, the natural and supernatural, and many other areas of thought and life, all began to move further and further away from each other until the divide became, it would seem, an infinity. The divide would eventually lead to the shipwreck of the twentieth century, its many graveyards, and the modern sensibility. Yes, I know, it was more complicated than that—but still, I think there is some truth to those connections.

After all, once such a division is believed to be true, it doesn't make room for the material and the spiritual. All it does is leave the material. The spiritual becomes so abstract, so apart from anything we can know, all one is left with is deism or agnosticism/atheism. The ethical becomes something we can't specify and thus the technological becomes the mean. There is no basis for asking "should" we do something, but only "can" we do it. If we "can" we will. As Martin Luther King, Jr. noted, we end up with "guided missiles" used by "misguided" men.

We live in the flotsam and jetsam of those historical philosophical moves—moves that led the world at that time to ignore the lighthouse of one world. And thus the rocks beckoned like sirens, black, jagged, and hidden just beneath the surface. And so here we are, gazing up from the sandy bottom as the shimmering light shines down through the watery expanse.

But what has changed really? Nothing. Only our perception of the world. We simply "see" the world differently now. We imagine the world as split, divided. We do this with such hubris. We think we are grand cartographers. Having split the world in two, like atoms, we now set out to map our conquest. And in our mapping, we miss the glory in front of us.

As an aside, the fundamentalist/evangelical world reads their Bibles this way—as maps. We open and follow the directions. We note the longitude and latitude, north and south, east and west. We note distance and scale. There, see, it's right there and all who follow the map correctly will arrive at the same spot. And if they don't, they must have misread or missed an important directional clue or piece of information. Because, of course, we have our map and north, south, east, and west never change.

The task of our time is to "see" the world anew, to imagine something greater than what we have been told, to re-narrate the world as one world. As Maximus the Confessor told us:

> The world is one...for the spiritual world in its totality is manifested in the totality of the perceptible world, mystically expressed in symbolic pictures for those who have eyes to see. And the perceptible world in its entirety is secretly fathomable by the spiritual world in its entirety, when it has been simplified and amalgamated by means of the spiritual realities. The former is embodied in the latter through the realities; the latter in the former through the symbols. The operation of the two is one.[8]

And this one world doesn't give easily to being mapped or controlled—because it is not some dead thing.

OF BODIES, SOULS, PUZZLES, AND MAGIC

Much of the Christian life, of discipleship, of spiritual maturation, is learning to see, hear, taste, smell, and touch. It is not so much about learning new information. We often think we are maturing when we gain new information or knowledge. The problem, though, is that we, us, who we are, the person, the heart, remains the same—we have simply added another piece of information to our memory.

I'm all for obtaining knowledge and information. The many full bookcases in our house and my Kindle would all provide testimony in my favor. Reading, listening, taking in new knowledge and information makes a well-rounded person. This essay is information/knowledge. Again, I'm very pro-education, pro-reading, and for the obtaining of knowledge.

My point is that such *alone* is not what really changes us. The fallen powers and principalities spoken of by St. Paul in Ephesians have a great and extensive knowledge of the material world, scripture, and of matters both theological and philosophical. The devil quoted scripture and the demons believe in God. Still, this knowledge has not changed who they are.

Imagine one is putting a puzzle together. As we keep adding pieces, the picture becomes clearer. We finally add that last piece, sit back, and take in the whole picture. We see it in its totality; we feel a sense of accomplishment. We often think of spiritual maturity in the same way. We start putting the pieces together, tiny bits of information, each jigsaw of knowledge, until we have a good grasp of, or can perceive, the totality.

The problem is we can do that and still be the same person at the end as we were at the beginning. The puzzle didn't change us, and whether or not we can truly see or perceive the totality is actually questionable. The totality, the fact there are no more pieces, the fact it looks like the picture on the box, can tempt us into thinking we have mastered or understand the puzzle's picture. However, if we are not changed, then this may be an illusion. Such is always the possibility when thinking the piecing together of information or knowledge is the same as maturing spiritually or being able to perceive wisely.

We often attribute discipleship, spiritual growth, to the ability to solve theological puzzles. To the contrary, we are the puzzle that needs to be solved. Solving puzzles is wonderful, but while the puzzle was solved, we weren't. A person can go to work and be tasked with solving many puzzles. They may solve those. They may go home and be tasked with solving the puzzles their family puts before them. They may solve those too. At the end of the day however, they may lie in bed and be unable to solve the riddle, the puzzle of themselves.

My point is not that we can "solve" the puzzle of ourselves. "Solving" suggests a mastery and completeness we will not experience in this life. We are mysteries, and only in glory, in eternity, in union with the Holy Trinity could we ever say we will "know" as we are "known." Whether that amounts to "solving" I have no idea (I doubt it). My point is that the puzzle of who we are is where we start if we want the other puzzles of life to help us become more "put together," if you will. We need to be vulnerable and open to the puzzles of life, through all our senses, not just our cognitive faculties/reason, to allow those puzzles to help us with our own internal puzzles.

If we allow our senses to become sensitive to the created world, we can begin to "see" and perceive more of those aspects that can change us, not simply add to our store of knowledge. This is why the liturgy is so important. The liturgy, in worship, allows our entire body, all our senses, to be present and open to this world in its created, divine, and good nature. When we practice silence, or fast, we again allow the totality of our bodies to, in turn, allow creation, or the Wisdom of God, Sophia, to begin to fill in the missing pieces of the puzzles we are.

As we get a greater sense of the whole, of the picture of ourselves, we in turn can now see and perceive the created world better as well. As we change, while we may look out upon the same creation we did the day before, we now see it differently. What changed? The rocks are still where they were. The trees didn't move. We changed. Thus, all our senses open and present to creation, are now able to see what has always been there but was hidden from our "sight" or other senses.

Much of discipleship, of spiritual growth, in my view, is best summed up in a quote by Eden Phillpots: "The world is full of magic things, patiently waiting for our senses to grow sharper."[9]

The entire world lays open before us, but we can't "see" it. We can't sense it. The magic things (which I take to be the mediation of creation to us by Sophia—the Wisdom of God) don't lay themselves open to us through mastery by knowledge, but by allowing our senses (all of them) to grow sharper, which is what the liturgy, prayer, fasting, practicing silence, acts of mercy, and other spiritual disciplines allow to happen.

I mentioned *Sophia*. In the ancient Greek, the noun form of the word we translate as Sophia means clever, prudent, of sound judgment, and wise. Something older Christian traditions can offer us are ways of understanding that have been lost in modern times. In the Eastern Orthodox Christian tradition, they speak of a personification of the Wisdom of God. This is taken from scripture:

Wisdom cries out in the street;
   in the squares she raises her voice.
   At the busiest corner she cries out;
   at the entrance of the city gates she speaks:
   "How long, O simple ones, will you love being simple?
   How long will scoffers delight in their scoffing

and fools hate knowledge?

Give heed to my reproof;

I will pour out my thoughts to you;

I will make my words known to you (Proverbs 1).

There are other verses in the Bible that also speak of wisdom as feminine. Wisdom in scripture is often referred to in the feminine as if wisdom were a woman, a divine being or person. This person though is not a god or fourth member of the Trinity, she is something else. Even in the Orthodox tradition, what she is exactly is still discussed and debated.

Putting that aside, some of the Orthodox theologians[10] who wrote of Sophia describe her as the very created world or Mother Earth in a sense. This is also what makes the material/physical world alive. The world has wisdom to offer us if we will listen. It has often been noted that since the Industrial Revolution and the ascendancy of science and technology, that we have too often "raped" the earth. We have taken by force the resources therein, with no regard to the damage being done to our environment.

Given the thought of creation as feminine, that term "rape" especially takes on very disturbing and sobering connotations. I believe we need to recover, seek, and be open to the truth of Sophia, the divine feminine, Mother Earth. We shouldn't master, violate, use, despoil, or approach nature with violence. As with all things, we should approach creation with love and openness. When we commune with nature, we commune with Sophia, which is all contained in the Holy Trinity.

Communion brings connection. We have to be open to such though. Further, I would add that walking, swimming, feeling the sunshine on our faces, wind, rain, and dirt beneath us, and other connections to "real" environments as opposed to virtual ones, also facilitate this sharpening of our senses and helping us to be open. Finally, as created beings, it is also our openness to each other that allows for our senses to grow sharper.

When we can perceive the magic things again, such is an indication we are changing, maturing, and this comes from all our senses growing sharper, which is something that often happens in spite of any new information or knowledge gained or mastered cognitively/rationally.

Be open to creation. Be open to the magic of this world.

HELL WILL PROBABLY LOOK LIKE A THOMAS KINKADE PAINTING

Anyone familiar with Thomas Kinkade, whose paintings grace the walls of many older fundamentalist and evangelical churches, may wonder how his idyllic scenes of ivy-covered stone cottages, with nearby babbling brooks, green pastures, and light filled peaceful images could possibly be compared to hell.

It's merely a suspicion on my part, although it is drawn somewhat from Scripture. In 2 Corinthians,[11] we read that, "... even Satan disguises himself as an angel of light." I'm a bit suspicious of those drawn to overt, poorly done, "Christian" movies, which are often nothing more than propaganda, Kinkade paintings, G-rated movies (exclusively), Christian contemporary pop music, and worlds scrubbed clean, shiny, and bright. These are often the same people who wear on their sleeve the fact they don't drink, smoke, or chew, and don't care much for those who do. There is a purity here that doesn't impress me or strike me as, well, pure.

It seems deceptive to me. It doesn't look like anything real. It almost appears to be a rejection of creation, of life. The beauty of creation, of reality, or our lived lives—lies in the grandeur of the ordinary. Life, living, is sweaty, smelly, dirty, and wonderfully plain. Life is dirt, water, sun, air, grass, food, flesh, and each other in all our glory. That glory is glorious because it is real and ordinary. The attempt to paint over this very earthy, dirty, smelly, and real canvas, is an attempt to escape and deceive.

It's a disguise. Notably, this is what we are told Satan does. This fallen angel doesn't appear as something natural, plain, or ordinary. This entity appears as an, "angel of light." But the "attractiveness" here is a cover for something ugly. We think of angels and of light as mirroring what our culture has told us is beautiful and desirable. We have an idea in our minds (whether accurate or not), of what these angels and light should look like.

However, in Isaiah, Christians believe a picture of Jesus (God in the flesh) is given to us:

> "...he had no form or majesty that we should look at him,
>   and no beauty that we should desire him.
> He was despised and rejected by men,
>   a man of sorrows and acquainted with grief
>   and as one from whom men hide their faces
>   he was despised, and we esteemed him not."[12]

Here's the deal: I don't believe Kinkade would ever have painted the Jesus recorded here. And we don't really want to depict the person described in Isaiah. Why? Because this is a picture of a loser. This is the fellow who wanders into the party and all the popular people turn aside in embarrassment and whisper, "Who invited that guy?"

And yet, here is the King of the universe, the Savior of the world. The person described by Isaiah is normally shamed into leaving the party or even, in the case of Jesus, killed. He doesn't belong in our world—the one we are trying to create for the sole purpose of getting away from people like him. We are drawn to pictures like Kinkade's, so we can escape his (and the people like him) presence.

But the world we are trying to reflect in these paintings is fake. It's not real. It is a world that never existed and never will. We assume an ideal world is one where the dirt, the blood, the odor, the imperfect things, the embarrassing things, the awkward things, are all gone or hidden. It's the "Hallmark" channel world.

We want a world where children, family members with mental illness or disability, sit quietly and never make us feel embarrassed or awkward. God forbid our lawn, our car, our house, our clothes, our salary, our spouse, our children, or family ever, ever embarrasses us or make anyone feel awkward. That would be hell.

And so, we are drawn to the "angels of light" and to the painters of light, who create a world for us to hide within. Here everything is bright, clean, and pretty. Here we are all healthy, beautiful, tan, and happy. Here there is no embarrassment or awkwardness. Here all the dirtiness, earthiness, odor, sweat, blood, embarrassment, and awkwardness are painted over. We are left with something that sort of looks appetizing, like a Twinkie, but then ends up being, well, a Twinkie.

In such a hell, they will think they are in heaven (see, *The Good Place*[13]); it will be everything they always thought it would be. How could it be anything else? Just look at this picture! This must be heaven! And those in "hell" must be experiencing the very opposite—they will think. Hell must look the very opposite of a Thomas Kinkade painting, right? It probably looks like a slum, with broken-down shacks in a trash-filled lot. Picture garbage cans on fire for warmth.

And part of this imagined heaven that is really hell will be the satisfied joy of living in such a "beautiful" place while those "below" (or wherever they are) suffer in eternal torment. And part of that suffering, in their minds, will be having to reside in a place the exact opposite of their Thomas Kinkade world. A horrible world of common natural colors, plain vistas, imperfect scenes, with all the attendant feel and smells. An ordinary world. What a hell of a place, they will think.

And to them, their world of kitsch, of plastic serenity and syrupy lightness will be heaven. It will be a place where a man despised, unattractive, dirty, smelly, and bloody would never be found. Such a person, such a scene, would be, well, too messy, gloomy, and dark. We could hardly go on with our plastic, sun-filled lives, with such a Debbie-downer present. Certainly, such a figure belongs in the "other place."

Look, if we never wanted the Jesus described in Isaiah 53, then we will hardly want the resurrected Jesus who comes in all his glory. We might think we would, but blindness toward the one will lead to blindness to the other. The blindness comes from being distracted by, and staring at, shiny "angels of light."

If we can't recognize the *Pretty Woman*[14] who shops as a prostitute as opposed to the one who shops in all her recently attained wealth, then the problem is with us, not Julia Roberts, or Jesus.

And that is why I think hell, as traditionally understood, will look like a Thomas Kinkade painting.

A THEOLOGY THAT BLEEDS

In my former life as an evangelical (actually I was more of a fundamentalist), I was always interested in the debate over eternal security and whether or not one could lose their salvation. Even at the age of 13 or so, I would read anything I could find regarding the Calvinist/Arminian debate.[15] Yes, weird, I know. (This may explain a lot about my childhood…)

As an adult, and probably right before seminary, I became a fairly strident Calvinist. How, I wondered, was this not obvious to all Christians—that Calvin nailed it. This was the correct and only way, I surmised, to interpret scripture and understand the Christian narrative. Everything else was either heretical or just poor theology. Well, let's just say a lot has changed since then. Now, I have mostly the same view of Calvin as David Bentley Hart.[16]

This has been discussed elsewhere, but I think what attracted me to Calvinism was its systematic completeness and confidence. It was a whole circle. It encompassed everything, made sense of everything, with no remainder. It was a pretty box all tied up neatly and nicely with a bow on top. Of course, it was a pretty box full of horrendous suppositions, sort of like the scene in *Raiders of the Lost Ark* where they peer inside the beautiful gold ark only to have their faces melted off.

Many of us don't like loose ends. We don't like it when the puzzle is almost complete, only to find one or two pieces missing. We don't like the book or movie that ends with some questions unanswered, or where the meaning is ambiguous with no resolution. We like our mysteries solved. We are uncomfortable with the awkward silence that accompanies those moments when something slightly off and completely unexpected is said or done. We prefer our division equations to have no remainders. And Calvinism is perfect in that sense.

Here's the problem. There could hardly be a conception of the world further apart from reality than that. Life does have loose ends. Life has remainders; it has things left over and left behind. It has things that don't fit nicely into boxes. To say that life is messy and complicated is to state the obvious. Just when we think we have everything in place, we notice something missing, something not quite right, something askew. A person normally present is absent. There is an awkwardness between us that wasn't there before. A marriage falters.

Of course, Calvinism has an answer for all of the out-of-place things, the remainders, and all: God. God is sovereign and ultimately in charge of everything, from the movement of an atom to the implosion of a star. Whether the hand that helps one up, or the hand that slaps one's face, God is the prime and final mover.

"Sovereignty" becomes a synecdoche for God as pure will and motion. From the creation of existence, everything explodes out in streams of perfectly preconceived and predestined lines, now moving zombie like toward their intended target and goal, whatever they might be, and nothing can change their trajectory. Existence is simply physics and math. Think of God as pipe bomb, but completely in charge of each fragment. That this makes God the devil no Calvinist seems to notice. There is talk of a "permissive" will as opposed to a "perfect" will, but if it was our child's life taken away, if it was one of us walking into a gas chamber at Auschwitz, do such distinctions even matter? Does knowing it was the "permissive" type help us?

The idea of a permissive and perfect will is an attempt to provide a reason for the unreasonable, something intelligible for what is morally unintelligible. These are all remainders, the things left over or left behind. All these sorts of things don't fit into our equations and if we try and make them, we do the devil's work. Equations with no remainders, in the moral economy of God's goodness and love, is the devil's math. The death of a child (or any living thing) doesn't fit into a moral equation with no remainder, nothing left over.

What we see in modernity, with Western liberalism (meaning classic, not in any pejorative sense), is the attempt to build systems that are complete, whole, all encompassing (everything is mapped and graphed), and without remainder, nothing left over or left out. In many ways, this is commendable. However, in practice, it often ends up hiding or attempting to hide those who, for whatever reason still end up as a remainder, something left over and behind. And because this can call the entire system into question, these remainders are often pushed out of sight, out of the way.

We think of this as the margins—the edges. These are the loose ends. This is the other side of the tracks. This is the prison. This is the down-and-out part of town, skid row. This is where the factories lie silent and decaying. And where former employees now through opioids and other means, live in a painless dream state of days gone by. This isn't main street, but the alleyway. This is the people sleeping under freeways and on park benches. This is where a person knows their world is less somehow because of their skin color, birthplace, or gender. These are the losers (so-called) and lost. These are the punished and poor—the remainder.

And in such a world, in such economies, this is exactly where we find Christ. Christ takes his place with the remainder, with the left over, the left out, and the left behind. Such is God's math and God's economy in a broken world. Look now, there he is. With the wounded and scarred, there he hangs, on the cross —outside the city, outside the camp. With arms stretched out, he embraces the captive, the down-and-out, the poor, the oppressed, and the lost. He takes in the whole world, as remainder. God doesn't explain to us, God dies with us.

Only then can we talk of resurrections.

Rather than tight, neat, crisp, and even theologies of cosmic balance, with no skin in the game, with no remainder, we need messy, complicated, and mystical theologies of a beautiful and loving attention to the remainder. We need theologies that bleed right along with the left over, the left out, and the left behind. If our theologies don't hang on crosses right next to those already hanging, of what good are they? Only such theologies, I believe, are worthy of the God they try and articulate.

THE ANARCHY OF LOVE

I came across these three words ("anarchy of charity") while re-reading David Bentley Hart's seminal theological work, *The Beauty of the Infinite: The Aesthetics of Christian Truth*, in the chapter on eschatology.[17] I immediately fell in love with those three words, even though I wasn't completely sure why I felt that way or what it was they conveyed. Those three words completely interrupted my reading. I was brought to a halt by their poetic power and what they stirred within me.

The expression was used in the context of justice. Hart can be very difficult to understand if one is not a professional (or at least, intelligent) philosopher or theologian. Thus, I could very well be misreading him. Still, in my reading, the idea seems to be that without a future end, judgment, closure, or summing up, any justice in the current moment can become problematic. Further, that said judgment or closure has already happened, is happening, and is also yet to come.

For Christians, the eschaton—the end—isn't only some future event, but an event that because of the birth, death, and resurrection of Christ, is both happening now and yet comes to us again and again in every moment. Thus, Hart writes:

> To turn from the eschatological is to close off the present within economy, to move from the radical event of judgment to the rooted stability of institution, to become resigned to the limiting measures that ignore the call, and the threat, of the infinite; to forget that the eschatological verdict has been pronounced already, within history, and has raised up the crucified, is to resist the anarchy of charity.[18]

Again, perhaps I have misread Hart's meaning here as to the entire context or have not done it justice. However, allow me to digress. I want to focus on those three words, the "anarchy of charity." In my mind, they speak in so many ways. As I paused to reflect upon those words, here is where those reflections took me.

First, several Bible passages came to mind:

"But the fruit of the Spirit is love, joy, peace, patience, kindness, goodness, faithfulness, gentleness, self-control; against such things there is no law" (Gal 5:22).

"Teacher, which is the great commandment in the Law?" And he said to him, "You shall love the Lord your God with all your heart and with all your soul and with all your mind. This is the great and first commandment. And a second is like it: You shall love your neighbor as yourself. On these two commandments depend all the Law and the Prophets" (Matthew 22:36-40).

"...For Christ is the end of the law for righteousness to everyone who believes" (Romans 10:1-4).

"And he carried me away in the Spirit to a great, high mountain, and showed me the holy city Jerusalem coming down out of heaven from God...and its gates will never be shut by day— and there will be no night there..." (Rev 21).

I pondered the difference between a culture or civilization defined by a plethora of laws and one defined by anarchy. Anarchy seems scary to us and often, rightly so. It feels very unsafe and even violent. We picture the apocalypse, *Mad Max*, *The Walking Dead*, or even the American West of the 1800s, when what are now states were only territories.

The word *anarchy* is normally applied in the context of government, rule, or organization; it is the lack, thereof. We might picture the cries of politicians for "law and order" transposed against a gathering, for instance, like Woodstock or Bohemian enclaves. I'm reminded of the 1953 film, *The Wild One* with Marlon Brando. It's a story about a rebellious motorcycle gang causing havoc in a small town. When Brando's character is asked what he's rebelling against, he responds, "Whaddaya got?"

Many of us are old enough to remember a time when people didn't lock their doors at night and were comfortable leaving their keys in their cars. Children could roam freely and much of the violence we hear about or experience now was uncommon. I realize this may have been true in more rural than urban locations, but still, there was a difference. I understand no historical time-frame was ideal or without its own peculiar trouble, but I hope my point is taken.

We might want to consider two trajectories as to government. The trajectory of more laws, rules, procedures, guidelines, and enforced structure may be a sign of civilizational failure. I note this not as an opponent of "big government," but merely to suggest it portends a deeper—much deeper—problem.

The other trajectory is risky. Rather than an ever-expanding web of laws and rules, it seeks a space where the -anarchy of charity- is let loose to provide, not legislated or outwardly enforced boundaries, but ones only the conscience can provide. The borders that are maintained come from an inner sense of character and integrity, a moral compass and governor. Yes, I know this is utopic and unrealistic.

We still live in a fallen world. There are indeed people in this world and life who, for whatever reason, may wish us harm. There are people who operate out of a sense of violence. I know we need a certain amount of law and order in this life. A broken world produces broken people, people who have been hurt. And people who are hurting, often hurt others. I get the need for law and boundaries.

I suppose my point is that when charity rises, the need for laws and enforced structure recedes. I believe this to be true for the individual as well. When we begin to operate more out of charity and less out of fear and rote obligation, we become truly free. No outside law or authority over us is needed. We begin to operate less from a patchwork of outward do's and don'ts, and more from an inner law of love that seeks only our neighbor's good, for no reason other than their wellbeing.

The kingdom brought by the life, death, and resurrection of

Christ, the life of the church now, and the kingdom to come are economies defined by the *anarchy of charity*. Whether or not we can ever truly obtain such in this life, I believe we should still work toward that goal, both individually and corporately.

It is why we pray, "Your kingdom come, on earth as it is in heaven." When the new Jerusalem comes down, it's gates are always open and never locked. The anarchy of charity has no need for locked doors, gates, or walls. May it be so.

CHAPTER SIX

MY PERSONAL RECONSTRUCTION

"If you continue to carry the bricks from your past, you will end up building the same house." —Unknown

Everyone coming out of the fundamentalist/evangelical world can take many paths from there forward. Some may become atheists or agnostics. Some may join another non-Christian faith or religion. Some may become a "none" where they do not identify with any faith and perhaps not even atheism. We are all different. I don't bring any judgment either way. Here is my prayer and hope for everyone on this path: That they find fulfilment, joy, peace, and love in their life. I pray they live in such a way their neighbor is loved and never harmed. That's not a bad life to live, no matter what one believes.

However, I would like to share my own personal story as to what helped me out of the fundamentalist/evangelical world, what helped me deconstruct, and then reconstruct my faith and theology. This path may not be for everyone. I'm not suggesting it as a blanket, one-size-fits-all type of path that will answer all s questions and meet their every need. Nope. I don't even know what that would look like.

I do know what helped me though. I share that now only as an option for the reader to consider—a basic first step. What helped me tremendously at first was reading outside the fundamentalist/evangelical world of well-known or popular writers, whether of the devotional or academic type. I've always been a reader, so that part was easy. If you are a reader, then get the audio versions and listen. I had to expand my limited knowledge base and get out of the echo chamber of that world, to even begin to imagine a different one.

Secondly, develop some deep personal relationships with others who are on the same journey or who have made their way out. Or, develop relationships with those who were never in that world but are familiar enough with it to understand where you are coming from. A tremendous help to me was an Episcopalian priest (Fr. Tom) who, because he was part of an evangelical home-schooling group of families, including ours, understood their views and theology very well.

Through that priest, I then met others who were outside the fundamentalist/evangelical paradigm. I was then exposed to different theologies and ways of looking at the world. This was challenging and curiosity inducing at the same time. It also helped to actually know people who had different theologies, and realize they were intelligent, decent, kind, and reasonable people. They were not the bogeymen I had too often been led to believe they were.

To sum up, read well and read outside your tradition. Make friends with and spend time with people outside the echo chamber in which you grew up. Unless you just have an epiphany, a moment of clarity, it normally takes time to get enough distance from the constructs we lived in to then look back and see them differently. Expanding our knowledge and community base will help provide that distance. This may seem very obvious, very simple, but it is a very basic first step forward toward finding the doors with the exit signs above them.

Normally we go through a deconstruction process because of some defining event, whether sudden or whether more of a slowly gathering storm. For me it was a slowly gathering storm. I began to realize I was no longer comfortable, even safe, in the religious world of my youth and young adulthood. I wasn't physically abused in any way. I wasn't treated badly per se— after all, I was a white male! No, it was more an alienation. It was more a process of looking around and realizing I fit in less and less.

I was beginning to see the world differently. And what I mean by "world" was everything: nature, my faith, religion, science, culture, politics, history, the arts, theology, doctrine, education, and any other area one cares to name. I wasn't just moving the furniture around in the old paradigm (Southern Baptist fundamentalism/evangelicalism), I was leaving the furniture there and looking for the exit door. It was a paradigm shift. Once that happened, it became almost impossible to remain in the world I was shifting away from.

Here is what helped me reconstruct once I found the exit. Again, I'm not saying this is the path for everyone. What I can say is that it is the path that helped me tremendously and still does. The path that helped me was the Eastern Orthodox Tradition. You can do some online searching for more information and at the end of this chapter there will be a list of books you can read to learn more about this tradition.

We often think of the ancient Christian faith as Western as opposed to the Eastern religions/traditions such has Buddhism, Hinduism, Sikhism, or Middle Eastern religions such as Islam or Judaism. However, Christianity is also a Middle Eastern religion in origin. The oldest, most ancient form of Christianity is Eastern. The liturgies, the teachings, the practices of the Eastern

Orthodox Church go back to those first few decades and centuries after the death of Christ.

Does that make it the true and only faith? No. But it doesn't hurt. Something I heard my entire young life in the fundamentalist/evangelical world was that we were just like the church of Acts. Our Pentecostal and Charismatic brothers and sisters disagreed! We thought we had bypassed all the failed history of the Roman church up to the Reformation and were now, or very close to, New Testament churches. Well, let's just say that was quite a stretch and quite a boast.

If you are truly looking for a Christian tradition that has the oldest historical footprint and can actually trace what they do, practice, and believe back to the earliest centuries of the Christian faith, it is the Eastern Orthodox tradition. Now, I write all this as someone who is not officially Orthodox. As of this writing, I have not been baptized into or accepted as a member of their church. Maybe I will one day. I don't know at this juncture. My point however is that this tradition and theology provided the skeleton upon which I could reconstruct my Christian faith. It was the paradigm that helped me leave the fundamentalist/evangelical world.

Having said that, let me also point out I think the Eastern Orthodox tradition has it faults. It is not perfect; no tradition or denomination is. Please don't leave whatever world you now inhabit faith-wise, thinking the next one is going to be perfect and without its own faults, failures, and ghosts. Remember this: We take our troubles with us. Often, it's not "them," it's us. We may need to look in the mirror if we find we are continually unhappy and unsatisfied no matter where we are. Sometimes we are the common denominator.

Along with Eastern Orthodoxy (EO), I would also suggest delving into and learning more about the Episcopal tradition, the Anglican tradition, and the Methodist tradition. I think these traditions too- will help you reconstruct your faith and theology and point you in a much more positive direction.

With those caveats and qualifications in mind, let me go a little further into how the Eastern Orthodox (EO) tradition provided the framework or skeleton upon which I could rebuild after the process of deconstructing. Obviously, I cannot, with any true justice, expound upon the entire Eastern Orthodox Tradition in one chapter—a myriad of books and entire tomes have failed to do such.

I'm going to speak to only three areas, which I think may be of some help to those who have come out of the fundamentalist/evangelical world. In addition, I will add three areas that were provided to me by friends who are familiar with both the fundamentalist/evangelical world and Eastern Orthodoxy. Upon my request, they were kind enough to provide me with three areas they wished more fundamentalists/evangelicals were aware of as it pertained to EO.

First, the three areas from EO that helped me the most in reconstructing my faith, theology, and spiritual life:

INTO THE MYSTIC

"Christianity is in the first place an [Eastern] religion, and it is a mystical religion." —Jean-Claude Barreau

I grew up in a fundamentalist/evangelical world that valued a systematic, rational, and almost scientific view of the Bible and the Christian narrative. We valued apologetics and the ability to defend the Bible from atheism and scientific views we felt undermined the Bible's accuracy or truthfulness. We were anxious to show the evidence that "demanded a verdict."

I don't know if it was a sort of insecurity on our part, but we needed people to know that our faith was one any intelligent, rational, reasonable, educated, and scientific person could hold without any shame.

What this reveals is just how modern we were. It actually reveals that the Enlightenment understanding of truth had won the day. We were now playing by its rules and trying to win on the field it had built. Such is a losing proposition however, all the way around. Once one agrees the field of play is the true and only field of play, the game is already lost. It was a field of play and a game the church never had any business playing. Instead, the church should have spent more time just unmasking the false nature of the field and the game itself.

That is exactly what fundamentalists/evangelicals failed to do. Instead, they decided to play an imaginary game on the false field provided by the "winners" of history (at that time anyway). This led to a type of faith and spirituality that was heavily weighted toward the cognitive, the intellect, the abstract, and the mastery of knowledge.

The problem for me became when none of that made much of a difference in my actual experience of life and living. After a while, the fact I could recite a scripture verse for whatever the problem or issue might be didn't seem to matter that much. The fact I could use the Bible like a reference book or encyclopedia didn't matter when there was no experience of the divine.

It was through the influence of EO and other older liturgical traditions that I was exposed to another way of being. And that way was mysticism. Before I delve into that a bit, let me make this point: There is nothing wrong with a reasonable, rational, and intellectually deep faith. There is nothing wrong with using one's intellect, reason, and logic as a part of that faith. And there need be no conflict or opposition between one's faith and the very best science or in the findings of any area of inquiry or knowledge.

Those who read "mystical" as "feeling" or "emotion" alone are not being fair. The mystical does not preclude intellect, reason, logic, or rationality. What it does, however, is position those aspects and interrogate them.

There has to be balance. It has to be both the head and heart. We need both love and reason. We need both a cognitive and experiential component to our faith. For me, this balance was missing in the fundamentalist/evangelical world I grew up in and that formed my understanding of the Christian faith and narrative. It very much, in my experience, slanted in one direction.

The Christian faith/religion/narrative is not a modern scientific worldview. It is not a set of rules or abstract philosophy. It is not a set of laws. It is not a systematic theology or a set of logical bullet points of propositional assertions. It is not a body of pure knowledge or statements of mere empirical fact. It may contain aspects of all those and it may be spoken of using some of those frames of reference. However, ultimately, I believe it is a mystery that first has to be experienced.

Fundamentalism breeds the need for certainty. It creates a sensibility that sees the world, not in color, but in black and white. There are no shades of gray. For instance, when it comes to the Bible, it must harmonize, it must be consistent, it must be logical, and most importantly, it must be mastered cognitively/rationally. There is little room, if any, for mystery in fundamentalism (evangelicalism too).

An aspect of the EO view is that much of our faith, our theology, our understanding of the Christian narrative is mysterious. We live within this mystery. It's okay if there is much about God and our faith that we do not understand completely or if we are uncertain about many of its elements. This allows for a deep humility. It is the realization that what we think we might know about God, the Bible, and the Christian narrative is like a drop in the ocean.

The mystical opens the door to the experiential. It allows for our entire being, not just our intellect or reason, to experience and know God. This is something the liturgical nature of worship helps facilitate. If one has ever attended an EO service or a high liturgical worship service, they hopefully know what I mean. The entire atmosphere, the building, the icons, the candles, the incense, the artwork, the chanting, the prayers, and movement of bodies is a conduit for us to experience the mystery of Christ, through the Holy Spirit, as we worship God the Father.

There is a wonderful and deep abiding beauty in the mystical, in the very mysterious nature of our faith and God. This has to be experienced fully, not just intellectually or through trying to master a body of information/knowledge. Beginning to grasp this truth and live within it was a tremendous help to me on my journey out of fundamentalism/evangelicalism.

THE COSMIC SCOPE OF SALVATION

The focus of modern, Western, American, Protestant fundamentalism/evangelicalism when it comes to salvation, is on the individual. Each person, at some moment in time, has to personally "receive" Christ as savior. They need to pray something like the "sinner's prayer." They confess they are a sinner, that Christ died for their sins, and they are now placing their trust and faith in Christ as savior. They are then to make this known publicly and be baptized.

This is the entire point of "altar calls" and the emphasis on evangelism in the fundamentalist/evangelical world. In fact, the line of thought is something like this: The physical world is eventually going to be destroyed by God, those who have confessed Christ will be "raptured" away, and then each will meet their eternal fate, whether heaven or hell. Thus, it really is all about the individual and their "relationship" with Christ. That is all that ultimately matters.

If one has ever wondered how it is that Americans are so

individualistic, concerned about their personal autonomy, rights, and liberties, but correspondingly suspicious of the collective, community, state, or institution, they need look no further than this underlying view of salvation.

This view of salvation, which is modern and Western, something drawn more from the Enlightenment than the Christian narrative, is about distinct and separate objects in space, with no link or connection to other distinct and separate objects in space. They can come into contact and interact with each other, but there is no deeper connection.

EO and most other Christian traditions take a completely different view. In their view, everything is connected because everything exists in Christ.

"He is before all things, and in him all things hold together" (Colossians 1:17).

Whether or not one is a Christian, by way of creation their physical nature, their soul, is held together in Christ. Thus, everything is connected through Christ. And this doesn't only apply to humans. "All things" means...*all things.*

It means existence. It means the cosmos, from our earth to the farthest reaches of the universe. It means the elements, fire, water, earth, and air. It means the oceans, mountains, rivers, and trees. It means every animal. All things are held together and grounded in Christ. Thus, again, everything is connected—there is relationship. A rock is not simply a rock or a tree, a tree. We are all part of a tapestry that is Christ.

Ours is not a compartmentalized universe/existence, with an upper compartment (heaven/spiritual) and a lower (earth/material) compartment. Rather, there is a deep connection between all things, both material and spiritual, via Christ.

When Christ died on the cross, the entire cosmos died with him. When Christ was raised from the dead, the entire cosmos was raised with him. Salvation was cosmic. It is not an individual matter. We may come to it as individuals—we awaken, we realize, we become aware of our salvation. But our salvation is already a fact. Salvation doesn't begin when I make some sort of verbal or heart-felt announcement. I simply become aware at some point that I was always a part of the Father's Kingdom. Like the prodigal, it's just that I came to myself and returned home. But that home, my relationship with the Father, was always there, a fact, a truth. And we all belong to that same Father and Kingdom.

Learning this, and more importantly, experiencing it, made a huge difference in my reconstruction. Rather than living what too often turned into a selfish existence, I was able to see the importance of community and fellowship. It's not about just "me." And that community and fellowship extended even to the physical environment, animals, and all of creation. It even extended to my enemies.

WHAT HAPPENED ON THE CROSS?

The third and final area that helped me (although there were many others) out of the fundamentalist/evangelical world, was encountering a different way to view what happened on the cross.

What exactly did happened on the cross? First, backtracking a bit, as we noted with my first point, the cross is a mystery to be experienced, before it is ever something to try and comprehend intellectually. In this life, I doubt it's even possible to know "exactly" what happened that day.

As most Christian readers will know, there are many theories of what happened on the cross as it pertains to our (and cosmic) salvation. These are called theories of atonement. I'm not going to go into each one, but just for example there is the moral influence theory of atonement, the ransom theory, the satisfaction theory, and many more. Please research those and others to gather more information on how the church, and different parts of the church, have tried to articulate what happened on the cross over the centuries.

I want to focus, however, on the theory of atonement held by many (if not most) fundamentalists and evangelicals. It is called the penal substitutionary theory (PSA). Before leaving that world, it was also the theory I held, believing it to be the most biblical and accurate explanation for what took place as to our salvation.

In a nutshell, PSA puts forth the idea that sin must be punished. It can't simply be forgiven and made to go away. Our sin, our nature, makes us the enemies of God. In our sinful state, God hates us. We deserve nothing but God's wrath, his punishment. Thus, what to do? We can't save ourselves. We are "dead" in our sins. God then sends his Son, who takes the punishment in our place. God pours out his wrath upon his own Son so that we might have life.

The fact this makes God look very much like the pagan gods of old seems to get by a lot of people. It makes God look like the sort of deity that needs blood, needs a sacrifice or he's going to get very angry. This is the picture of an angry, bloodthirsty god, and not the God of either Testament.

PSA arose out of a Western, Roman, and Reformation ethos. The focus of this theory is law, the courtroom, and the matter of punishment. As noted here:

> In Western Christianity, Christ is seen as the one who suffers the punishment human beings deserve for their sins. Christ is seen as victim. By contrast, in Eastern Christian thought, Christ is the victor: he defeats those enemies and frees humanity from their bondage.[1]

And Christ does this not only through the cross, but by his incarnation, death, and resurrection. He is the second and last Adam. All these aspects are important, critical even, to our salvation and the salvation of all things. Rather than seeing the cross as some sort of legal exchange to appease the wrath and anger of God, it is seen as one aspect of God's triumph over sin, death, the devil, and the powers of hell.

This new (to me) understanding of atonement, salvation, was extremely helpful to me. The fact it was older than the PSA and seemed to be supported by the grand sweep of Scripture, from beginning to end, rather than some proof texts, was also telling. This made much more sense to me and it also allowed me to see God in a brand-new light.

Rather than a God made in the image of the blood thirsty and easily offended gods of pagan lore, this was a God who fit the very picture of Jesus on earth. His anger on earth was only ever directed at the religious and political people of his day who spent too much time making the lives of the "least of these" more miserable and more difficult than they already were.

Rather than an angry deity calling out for blood and death, this God cried out, "Father, forgive them..." The cross wasn't a revelation of God's anger or need for satisfaction, it was a glorious triumph of love and forgiveness. At this, all the powers of sin, hell, and death were defeated and trampled down. There was no power opposed to God, then or now, that could stand after such an event, a rupture, an apocalyptic fissure of existence displaying an infinite, sublime, breathtakingly beautiful, lavish, and extravagant love.

These three areas, the mystical nature of the Christian faith and narrative, the cosmic scope of salvation, and a better understanding of what happened on the cross were critical to my reconstruction. Maybe these three areas don't resonate with you like they did me. Maybe you knew this already. Again, this is just my own story, my own experience. It may be there are other areas, other truths, other paths, that will better resonate with you and be more helpful.

My whole point here is that if you end up walking away from

fundamentalism/evangelicalism, if you need to deconstruct your faith and history, there are other paths, tools, people, churches, books, institutions, and resources to help you make that journey in a positive, encouraging, and helpful way. There are a myriad of resources now to help you reconstruct and rebuild your spiritual life.

No one has to make this journey on their own. In fact, that would probably be the worst way forward. We were made for community. We need spiritual direction, discipleship, and friendship. We need accountability. I don't believe we are saved on our own or by ourselves. I believe I need others for my salvation. I believe you need others for your salvation. We are saved together.

I have three wonderful friends who have backgrounds in both the evangelical world and the EO world. One, Pastor Bill Berry, is a retired evangelical pastor. Later in life however, he was drawn to EO and incorporated much of its theology/liturgy/prayers into his life and beliefs. The other, a woman, also came from an evangelical background, but eventually was baptized and became Orthodox. Part of her ministry is painting icons. She would like to remain anonymous. Finally, Mr. David Quilici was also raised in the evangelical tradition and has served as a worship leader and held other leadership positions in that world as well. He too has since become Orthodox and is currently a sub-deacon. I want to thank them each for their contributions here (Please note: Their contributions are not an endorsement of every single other thing I have written in this book—they only apply to this chapter and my specific question to them). Here is the question I asked them to address: What are three aspects of EO you wished more fundamentalists/evangelicals were aware of?

I am going to paraphrase their responses to me; I hope I do their thoughts justice! Again, I hope the reader will take these as areas for further investigation and reflection. Perhaps these areas will be the ones that resonate with the reader, strike a deep chord, and help them reconstruct their faith away from fundamentalism/evangelicalism and toward something more positive and redemptive.

Pastor Bill Berry:[2]

1. The purpose of all creation and redemption is for the purpose of bringing us into complete union/participation in the life of the Father and the Son and the Holy Spirit, so that we might truly be filled with the fullness of God and partakers of the divine nature. Thus, we love as He loves; we care for creation as he cares for creation.

2. The teaching that all of life is rooted in the trinity and the incarnation. These are not theological ideas to be argued, but the foundation for all of life. This also reveals the paradoxical nature of God, which in turn reveals the paradoxical nature of all creation and life.

3. The belief that the holy mysteries (eucharist/baptism/sacraments) are a means for me to personally encounter the living God of the universe, which allows me to experience him through union with Him. (knowing).

Anonymous:

1. God is actually not angry with us. God is infinite love, mercy, and Holiness.

2. True worship requires the training of the heart to surrender to God's silence.

3. Christianity is not primarily a moral upgrade. Living a moral life and "following rules" are the guardrails that are meant to lead us into a lifetime practice of communion... communion with God, communion with each other, communion with Creation, and communion with the Saints.

Mr. David Quilici:

1. *We can be connected to the historic church—the Church of the book of Acts.* What was the church from the book of Acts like? Every Protestant church I was a part of was trying to respond to that question. And every church answered it differently. The Apostle Paul gave us some clues on how to answer this. He wrote to Saint Timothy, "If I am delayed, you may know how one ought to behave in the household of God, which is the church of the living God, the pillar and bulwark of the truth" (1 Tim. 3:15). Note that he writes that it's the Church that is "the pillar and bulwark of the truth." Passages like this made me wonder which church has stood the test of time on doctrine and has millions of martyrs testifying for the last 2000 years.

Likewise, the Apostle Paul writes, "So then, brethren, stand firm and hold to the traditions which you were taught by us, either by word of mouth or by letter" (2 Thess 2:15). After being founded by the Apostle Peter, the church of Antioch sent out the apostles Paul and Barnabas. I belong to the Antiochian Orthodox Church, which traces its lineage back to that same local church in Antioch. The Orthodox Church has indeed maintained the traditions as taught by word and letter. Being able to read the descriptions of the services and theology of the early church (such as the Didache, St. Justin Martyr, and St. John Chrysostom), and know we are still celebrating those same services, all while holding the same theology—is a joy beyond words.

2. *Learning to Pray.* Learning to pray, truly and ceaselessly was something I long desired as an evangelical. But trying to pray what came to mind or "what was on my heart" often left me distracted. The deep tradition of prayer and the prayers them- selves have been great aids. Orthodox Prayer books provide a wonderful means of deeply reverent and devotional prayers for many occasions. Having a framework for morning and evening prayers has been profoundly impactful in my journey. It also provides the added benefit of common prayer for a family. Being

able to have morning and evening prayer time, in which even children can participate, has been transformational.

   3. *Experiencing Tradition and Theology.* Tradition does not have to be stale. Theology doesn't have to be merely academic. There is so much more. The Orthodox Church believes that she has maintained the true faith handed down from the Apostles, as revealed by the Holy Spirit. The Orthodox Faith is to be embodied and lived, not preserved as an antique in a museum displayed behind glass. Instead, faith is rooted in the revelation and living experience of God in the context of the unity of the Church. The doctrines and theology of the Church are not merely formulas or theories and speculations, but instead require active participation in the prayers, services, and sacraments of the Church. "If you are a theologian, you will pray truly. And if you pray truly, you are a theologian."[3]

I believe all three point out some very helpful and interesting aspects of EO and how it applies to fundamentalism/evangelicalism. My sense is that many who are either EO or find themselves on the same page as EO theologically, would most likely agree with my three friends, in that, they too wish fundamentalists/evangelicals were aware of these differences.

   I can't stress this enough: EO was extremely important for my reconstruction and continuing faith journey. That is simply my experience. However, it may not be the path for you and that is okay. I offer it here only as one option among others. All I suggest is that you look into it, investigate, research, read, reflect, and get to know some EO priests or parishioners.

   Here is the main point: Once one leaves the fundamentalist/evangelical world, there are resources and people who can help them reconstruct and rebuild their faith, theology, and spiritual life. Please do not journey alone. And please don't think you either have to return to that world or wander aimlessly with no guidance or help. Neither is true.

EPILOGUE

Again, to walk away from fundamentalism or evangelicalism doesn't have to mean walking away from Christ or the Christian narrative. It doesn't have to mean one no longer believes the Bible or the core beliefs stated in the oldest Christian creeds and put forth by the early councils. It doesn't have to mean one has left the faith, backslid, rebelled, or is now an enemy of the faith. And don't let anyone ever tell you it has to mean any of those things. Those are only their own false perceptions.

Walking away means different things to different people, both for the person doing the walking and those on the outside observing the walking. But the people on the outside observing, do not get the last word on your own inner experience. Only the person doing the walking can have the last word, because only that person knows where they are right now and where they may be headed. *We* get to define what our own journey means to us, not what it looks like to an outside observer—especially if that observer is still standing on the same ground we just walked away from.

And I know for myself that leaving that world had nothing to do with leaving Christ or the Christian faith. In fact, for me, *it was because* of Christ and my faith that I needed to leave that world. It was necessary for my spiritual growth and formation. It was necessary for my spiritual, emotional, and mental health as well. In my opinion, fundamentalism/evangelicalism is not healthy, in any sense of the word.

I will say this: If that world was one's introduction to Christ and the Christian narrative, then wonderful. My concern though is that after that, it can often form toxic Christians who, I believe, end up with a very truncated and shallow view of the Christian narrative and faith. So, for me, it's still a terribly mixed bag. And again, I know there are good people in those worlds. I know they feel in their hearts and minds that they love Jesus. I get that. I recognize it and respect it. Sadly, I believe their view of Jesus and the Christian narrative to be warped and bent. I just know it was a place I could no longer live.

And I'm assuming that most of those reading this feel the same way or are on the brink so to speak. To those I say, move. Stand up. Start walking. You don't have to stay in a place you know is not healthy, toxic even. Take that first step. We all know how any journey begins. First, it begins in our hearts and minds. And then, we stand and take that first step. Do it. Don't wait. Don't look back and wish you would have. Put this book down and start, metaphorically speaking, packing. The first day of the rest of your life, if you want it, can start right now and is waiting for you right outside the door.

Peace and grace to you.

I was reading of a young man, an evangelical, conservative, and intelligent, who had waded into the waters of progressive Christianity only to find it wanting. He eventually returned to his former world. That is fine, although lamentable in my mind.

However, one of his criticisms was that while he had "deconstructed," there were no materials to "reconstruct" with. He felt like everything had been torn down and he was left to sit in the rubble wondering what was next.

Well, it's no wonder he returned to his former world. I would counter that most of that was on him. There are plenty of resources, books, institutions, churches, and people out there to help one rebuild their understanding of faith and the Christian narrative. He just didn't avail himself of any of those. The following is a partial (hardly exhaustive) list of just a tiny fraction of those resources. Start wherever you need to, but please know there are many, many voices and resources out there to help you rebuild and reconstruct your Christian life. No one need walk this journey alone.

Some suggestions and resources then:

1. *Read the books by these authors:*

Brian McLaren
Donald Miller
Richard Rohr
Rachel Held Evans
Rob Bell
Brian Zahnd
Peter Rollins

When you are ready, read anything you can by David Bentley Hart; however, much of his writing can be somewhat difficult (for various reasons, but certainly not because of the writing style), but it is worth the time to learn how to read him. His serious works require some background knowledge and familiarity with theology, philosophy, and church history.

These are just good places to start—there are plenty of other progressive writers, pastors/priests, theologians, and philosophers out there. Search them out.

. . .

2. *For a further exploration of Eastern Orthodoxy, I recommend these resources to the reader:*

Clement, Olivier. *The Roots of Christian Mysticism* (New York: New City Press, 1993).

Clendenin, Daniel B. *Eastern Orthodox Christianity: A Western Perspective* (Grand Rapids MI: Baker Books, 1994).

Gillqiust, Peter E. *Becoming Orthodox: A Journey to the Ancient Christian Faith* (Ben Lomond CA: Conciliar Press, 1989).

Hart, David Bentley. *The Beauty of the Infinite* (Grand Rapids MI: Wm. B. Eerdmans, 2003).

Payton, James R. Jr. *Light from the Christian East* (Downers Grove Il: Intervarsity Press, 2007).

3. *Organizations:*

https://progressivechristianity.org/partner-organizations/

4. Churches/Denominations:

https://www.progressivechristiansuniting.org/

5. Readers are welcome to reach out to me at: d.rocking415@gmail.com and also please see: https://www.patheos.com/blogs/divergence/

NOTES

ACKNOWLEDGMENTS & DEDICATION

1. In memory of Fr. Thomas Preston Brindley (1952-2021): Before this book went to print, my dear friend Fr. Tom left this life and became part of that great cloud of witnesses. We had discussed the fact I was writing a book and as always, he was encouraging and helpful. I must also include him in my dedication. I will miss him greatly. See you later my friend. Thanks for everything. *Donec obviam iterum.*

1. SAME FAITH—DIFFERENT PERSPECTIVE

1. Mark 9:24
2. 1 Peter 3:15
3. "Wikiquote," accessed February 3, 2021,
   https://en.wikiquote.org/wiki/Seraphim_of_Sarov
4. Sergius Bulgakov, *Unfading Light,* trans. Thomas Allen Smith, (Grand Rapids: Wm. B. Eerdmans, 2012), 30.
5. Deuteronomy 14:2
6. Ephesians 1:4
7. Romans 5:18
8. Colossians 1:19
9. Ephesians 1:10
10. Sergius Bulgakov, *The Holy Grail and the Eucharist* (Herndon: Lindisfarne Books, 1997).
11. Revelation 12:7

2. SALVATION AND THE END OF DAYS

1. Matthew 2:1
2. Acts 17:22-31
3. Matthew 25:31-46
4. 2 Samuel 12:7
5. Sergius Bulgakov, *The Bride of the Lamb* (Grand Rapids: Wm. B. Eerdmans, 2002), 515.
6. "Alexzandr Solzhenitsyn," Wikipedia, last modified March 10, 2021, https://en.wikipedia.org/wiki/Aleksandr_Solzhenitsyn.

7. Luke 15:11-32
8. Colossians 1:19
9. Gregory MacDonald, ed., *All Shall be Well: Explorations in Universal Salvation* (Cambridge: Lutterworth Press, 2011).
10. Hebrews 13:12
11. Hebrews 13:13
12. Genesis 6
13. Exodus 14
14. Daniel 3
15. Daniel 6
16. Psalm 23
17. Alistair W. Donaldson, *The Last Days of Dispensationalism: A Scholarly Critique of Popular Misconceptions* (Eugene, OR: Wipf and Stock, 2010).
18. Peter Rollins, *Insurrection* (New York, NY: Howard Books), 137.

3. THE BIBLE

1. https://www.abc.net.au/religion/how-to-read-the-bible-on-the-use-and-misuse-of-the-bible-in-the-/10095424
2. Matthew 23:15
3. Acts 17:6
4. https://en.wikipedia.org/wiki/Maginot_Line
5. https://en.wikipedia.org/wiki/Biblical_inerrancy
6. https://baptistnews.com/article/sbc-controversy-reverberates-for-second-third-generation-exiles-book-says/#.W2OXCtVKipo
7. Merold Westphal, *Whose Community? Which Interpretation?* (Grand Rapids: Baker Academic, 2009).
8. https://www.oxfordbibliographies.com/view/document/obo-9780195396577/obo-9780195396577-0340.xml
9. https://plato.stanford.edu/entries/truth-correspondence/
10. https://www.etsjets.org/files/documents/Chicago_Statement.pdf
11. Westphal, *Whose Community*, 20.
12. *Ibid*, 20.
13. James K.A. Smith, *Who's Afraid of Postmodernism?* (Grand Rapids: Baker Academic, 2006).
14. https://religionnews.com/2014/06/02/n-t-wright-bible-isnt-inerrantist/
15. https://www.dallasnews.com/opinion/commentary/2020/05/17/too-many-evangelical-christians-fall-for-conspiracy-theories-online-and-gullability-is-not-a-virtue/
16. Mark Noll, *The Scandal of the Evangelical Mind* (Grand Rapids: W.B. Eerdmans, 1994).
17. https://www.washingtonpost.com/lifestyle/magazine/jerry-falwell-jr-cant-imagine-trump-doing-anything-thats-not-good-for-the-country/2018/12/21/6affc4c4-f19e-11e8-80d0-f7e1948d55f4_story.html
18. Luke 21:1-4

19. Daniel 1:17
20. Matthew Barrett, "The Sufficiency of Scripture," Patheos, https://www.thegospelcoalition.org/essay/the-sufficiency-of-scripture

4. THE POLITICAL-CULTURAL

1. https://en.wikipedia.org/wiki/Life_Is_Beautiful
2. Brian Zahnd, *Postcards from Babylon* (USA: Spello Press, 2019).
3. Zahnd, *Postcards*, 37.
4. https://newrepublic.com/article/50754/calvin-and-american-exceptionalism
5. https://www.dallasnews.com/opinion/commentary/2018/06/07/first-baptist-pastor-robert-jeffress-gospel-of-division-does-not-represent-my-dallas/
6. 1 Peter 2:9
7. Mangina, Joseph L, *Revelation: Brazos Theological Commentary on the Bible*, edited by R.R. Reno. Grand Rapids: Brazos Press, 2010), 194.
8. Ephesians 6:12
9. Mangina, *Revelation*, 383
10. Mangina, *Revelation*, 466
11. Revelation 18:23
12. Luke 4:14-22
13. https://www.washingtonpost.com/national/on-faith/nt-wright-asks-have-we-gotten-heaven-all-wrong/2012/05/16/gIQAD4lTUU_story.html?utm_term=.54278c40b9e4
14. Arland J. Hultgren. *The Parables of Jesus* (Grand Rapids: Wm. B. Eerdmans, 2000).
15. *Ibid*, 321
16. *Ibid*, 321
17. *Ibid*, 322
18. *Ibid*, 324
19. *Ibid*, 318
20. *Ibid*, 322
21. https://www.politico.com/story/2019/08/12/trump-evangelicals-blasphemy-profanity-1456178
22. https://churchleaders.com/outreach-missions/outreach-missions-articles/331815-john-macarthur-on-social-justice-its-heresy.html
23. Matthew 25:40
24. Luke 4:16-21
25. https://www.patheos.com/blogs/eastmeetswestsocialworker/2019/03/biblical-justice-versus-social-justice/
26. Rob Bell, *Love Wins* (New York, NY: Harper One, 2011)
27. David Bentley Hart, *That All Shall Be Saved* (New Haven, CT: Yale University Press, 2019)
28. Luke 4:18-19

29. Frederick Nietzsche, *The Gay Science* (Mineola, NY: Dover Publications, 2020).

5. OPEN RANGE—THE POETIC

1. For a good non-academic understanding of modernity, see Stanley J. Grenz, *A Primer on Postmodernism* (Grand Rapids, MI: Wm. B. Eerdmans, 1998)
2. For a good understanding of disenchantment, the modern, and the secular see Charles Taylor, *A Secular Age* (Cambridge, MA: Belknap Harvard University Press, 2007).
3. https://en.wikipedia.org/wiki/Moonstruck
4. https://www.goodreads.com/quotes/537028-a-way-of-using-words-to-say-things-which-could
5. https://en.wikipedia.org/wiki/He_Stopped_Loving_Her_Today
6. https://en.wikipedia.org/wiki/Crazy_(Willie_Nelson_song)
7. John Milbank, *Theology & Social Theory* (Oxford, UK: Blackwell, 1993)
8. Oliver Clement, *The Roots of Christian Mysticism* (Hyde Park, NY: New City Press, 1993), 219.
9. https://www.goodreads.com/author/quotes/135803.Eden_Phillpotts
10. Sergei Bulgakov, *Sophia, The Wisdom of God* (Hudson NY: Lindisfarne Press, 1993)
11. 2 Corinthians 11:14
12. Isaiah 53
13. https://en.wikipedia.org/wiki/The_Good_Place
14. https://en.wikipedia.org/wiki/Pretty_Woman
15. https://en.wikipedia.org/wiki/History_of_the_Calvinist%E2%80%93Arminian_debate
16. https://www.clarion-journal.com/clarion_journal_of_spirit/2011/01/david-bentley-hart-on-calvin.html
17. David Bentley Hart, *The Beauty of the Infinite: The Aesthetics of Christian Truth* (Grand Rapids, MI: Wm. B. Eerdmans, 2003), 19Hyde Park, NY: New City Press, 1993), 399.
18. *Ibid*, 399

6. MY PERSONAL RECONSTRUCTION

1. James R. Payton Jr., *Light from the Christian East* (Downers Grove IL: Intervarsity Press, 2007), 122.
2. Pastor Bill Berry went to be with the Lord before this book went to print. He was a wonderful person, husband, father, grandfather, pastor, teacher, Christian, and friend.
3. Evagrius Ponticus, *Treatise on Prayer*, 61.

YOU MIGHT ALSO ENJOY...

LEAVING THE FOLD

By Marlene Winell

Have you been harmed by toxic religion?

Learn how to recover and reclaim your life.

Psychologist Marlene Winell is uniquely qualified to address the subject of this book. In addition to her personal experience with leaving fundamentalist religion, she has worked with clients recovering from religion for 28 years. She is known for coining the term Religious Trauma Syndrome.

Leaving the Fold is a self-help book that examines the effects of authoritarian religion (fundamentalist Christianity in particular) on individuals who leave the faith. The concrete steps for healing are useful for anyone in recovery from toxic religion.

Check it out today at: https://books2read.com/leavingthefold

Made in the USA
Las Vegas, NV
07 April 2022

46976695R00089